The Egg Man's Son

A San Francisco Irish Life

Kevin J. Mullen

"The Egg Man's Son: A San Francisco Irish Life," by Kevin J. Mullen. ISBN 978-1-60264-463-2.

Published 2009 by Virtualbookworm.com Publishing Inc., P.O. Box 9949, College Station, TX 77842, US.

Manufactured in the United States of America.

For Davitt and Christine

Introduction

One day in 1942, while on a shopping excursion with an adult family friend in what was then called the Eureka Valley, I noticed that the glass protecting the lever in the fire alarm box at 18th and Castro streets was missing. Any defense attorney worth his salt would doubtless call it an "irresistible impulse." I pulled the alarm as we walked by.

Within seconds, it seemed, the intersection filled noisily with fire equipment, the firemen looking about first for the fire, and then, angrily, for the damn kid who set off the false alarm. By then, though, I had made my way to the other side of the street with my unwitting adult accomplice. Who would suspect the little guy walking with a responsible adult, anyway?

Thirty-seven years later—and in a different life—I found myself at the identical location in the early morning hours of May 22, 1979, this time attempting to supervise a confusing mix of police forces and Gay rioters in the final phases of the White Night riot which followed on the manslaughter conviction of Dan White for the murder of Mayor George Moscone and Supervisor Harvey Milk.

At that moment I thought fleetingly that perhaps there is a divine providence, or karma, or whatever you want to call it, and that the balance sheet was being adjusted for my 1942 offense. What followed immediately was a watershed experience in my police career and my life.

As befits a San Francisco Irish story, mine starts in the Mission District in the 1930s (technically St. Joseph's Hospital on Buena Vista Heights); moves to the Inner Sunset in the late 1940s; and later to Daly City and Marin, while I remained connected with San Francisco institutions and people as a member of the police department.

It could be said that Irish interests had a prominent voice in governmental affairs at the time of my application to the police department. And I had all the necessary San Francisco credentials then much sought after in police candidates: Irish parentage, parochial schools, not too much egg-head education, successful military service, and experience with low-end physical jobs. On paper, I was their perfect candidate

For all of that, I got there by a rather circuitous route. Half-orphaned at five years old, I was raised for the most part in foster homes and Catholic boarding institutions, not an uncommon situation at the time. Many of my friends today shared similar experiences. I attended parochial grammar schools as did most Catholic children of the era where I was imbued—not always successfully—with the teachings of the church, religious and profane.

Also, like many young San Francisco Catholic males of my generation I spent time at St. Joseph's Junior Seminary in Mountain View, urged on there by the nuns and parents, ambitious for our intellectual and religious advancement. In my third year, I left and entered St. Ignatius High School from which I graduated in 1953.

Most of my classmates went on to college, as was expected of graduates of a college preparatory institution. Not me. I joined the army and spent three years in the American South and later Germany. Out of the army, I drifted for a couple of years, doing mainly laboring work, until by chance I came to the police department in 1959.

I didn't know it at the time—I don't know that anyone did—that urban America generally, and San Francisco in particular, was on the brink of a great social revolution that has yet to play itself out.

Over the course of my lifetime, San Francisco has gone from a city with an almost all white population to one where non-Latino whites are a decided minority. Its manufacturing base has largely departed and been replaced by tourist-centered employment. The old certainties about right conduct have been called into question and been replaced by a new and different set of civic dogmas.

At one time, San Francisco's saloons knew to shut down "voluntarily" from noon to three on Good Friday—if they knew what was good for them. It was a world in which Bishop Fulton Sheen could command an audience for a prime time network Sunday Evening show.

Now, San Franciscans bow their heads in hushed reverence as the Aids Quilt passes by. And the president of the San Francisco Police Commission is a transgender former executive of a sex toy company. It is truly a remarkably different place.

The San Francisco Police Department and its members both observed and participated in the changes that took place during the last half of the twentieth century, not always to everyone's satisfaction. Much of what has been written about the great changes that overtook San Francisco in that period has been from the perspective of those who brought about the "revolution" and have benefited from its victory.

My original purpose in putting together these thoughts was to leave a record to explain myself to my grandchildren when they become older and I am gone. Then I thought about the books and articles I have written which will survive me into a very different future. Even now, I realize I am out of step with some of the more "progressive" ideas which constitute contemporary thought in San Francisco. So here I will try to provide a context showing the circumstances under which my published ideas were formed.

Like all life stories, mine starts with the personal, for in early life we are all circumscribed by the small group of family members in which we find ourselves. Later, as our horizons broaden, we become involved with a wider spectrum of contacts and influences from the outside world. In my case, I happened to work for the San Francisco Police Department at a time of great social change in the city of my birth and thus, of necessity, became personally involved with many of the issues effecting that change.

At that point in my tale, the story shifts somewhat away from the personal and more toward professional considerations because that is what principally occupied me during those years. It was a serious time requiring a more serious tone than the relatively carefree period which preceded it.

This then is an attempt to provide a view of the city of the period—from the other side of the barricades, if you will—through one life lived during the last half of the previous century. I don't offer it as a definitive account of the period, or even a representative life, just my own personal journey through the city in an important, and, I hope, interesting time.

1 – Getting Started

Our mother died in 1940, just before Christmas. She was 38 and I had just turned five. Neighbors and friends gathered in the house at 570 30th Street as was the custom of the time. I remember a uniformed police officer among the mourners, an older cousin of my father's named Martin "Windy" Gallagher. We smaller children were bundled off that night to our Aunt Bridgie's house at 38th and Geary. It was dark, and I remember seeing the large lighted Christmas tree in front of McLaren Lodge in Golden Gate Park for the first time from the back seat of Uncle Ralph's big old square black sedan.

That same day Tait's at the Beach, the venerable resort on Great Highway at Ulloa Street which had introduced my immigrant relatives to San Francisco in the 1920s, burned to the ground in a mysterious fire. At the same time, Henry J. Kaiser opened his first shipyard at Richmond to fill British orders for ships, auguring our soon-to-be realized involvement in the world war. The old San Francisco was shedding its skin and giving way to the new.

Department store decorations were going up downtown and the advertisements were out for the last pre-war San Francisco Christmas. That year we didn't go downtown to see Santa Claus. Instead we whispered our lists into Aunt Bridgie's ear with the assurance that she would let Santa know of our desires. I asked for and received a stake-bed *Radio Flyer* wagon, red with white lettering.

My mother's people were Lynchs from Kilnarovanagh, not far from Macroon, in West Cork, Ireland. The earliest family reference I have been able to find was an entry in official documents recording taxes required of Catholics paid to the Protestant Church of Ireland. (Such telltales help explain the reasons behind our forebears' depth of faith, and their enmity toward those who might differ.) The document cited the birth of my great grandfather, Denis Lynch, in 1842. Denis married another Lynch, Ellen, with whom he had five children, one of whom was my grandfather, Humphrey, born in Ireland in 1865. The family moved to Massachusetts for a couple of years where another son was born. By 1867, Denis is recorded in the San Francisco City Directory as living on the grounds of Lone Mountain Cemetery. The family then settled on Collins Avenue between what was then called Point Lobos Road (Geary Boulevard) and St. Rose's Street (Anza).

As far as I can determine, all my people were working class. Denis worked as a cemetery laborer until his early death in 1880 and his son Humphrey, my grandfather, worked as a porter, then a guard, for the Wells Fargo Bank. In 1895, Humphrey married Galway-born Annie Finnerty at Holy Cross Church in San Francisco, and in 1902, their only child, Edna, my mother, was born.

When informed of my mother's death and that we were to be taken away, my immediate reaction was to regret that I wouldn't be able to see the hopscotch my sister Maureen had chalked on the sidewalk in front of the house that day. One of the women present at the wake commented on my apparent lack of emotion by saying I was too young to understand. I understood very well, and remember wondering at the time at the inappropriateness of my reaction. I realized later that it was the behavior of somebody who had already shut down. I suppose the psychological tool kit that would carry me through life was already in place.

Figure 1-Fat Kevin and Maureen ca. 1936

In general, I think I have earlier childhood memories than most. I was 14 months old in December, 1936 and I remember being fascinated by a glistening red ornament on the lower right-hand side of a Christmas tree, and everyone surrounding me getting noticeably excited as I moved to get it. I can fix the date because I was a very fat baby and didn't walk until I was 14 months old. That would have been Christmas of 1936. The excitement generated by those first steps is doubtless what imprinted the event in my mind.

For all my early recollections, I don't remember my mother as being present on the scene much. I don't have any memories of her ever being anything less than kind when she was present, but it seems she was absent a lot. She was afflicted with what the Irish call a "weak chest," some kind of bronchial/asthmatic condition which she has passed on to her children in some form or another. We didn't talk about the specific circumstances of her death growing up. A nun once told me brusquely that she died of "consumption." Her death certificate lists "myocardial insufficiency due to Bronchial allergic asthma due to toxemia of Allergic origin" as the immediate cause of death.

In any event, disabled by the condition which eventually carried her away, she was often in and out of hospitals and unable to care for us personally. I wince when I remember that I knew I could run away from her down the street because I knew she couldn't catch me due to her "condition." Kids can be cruel, or maybe it was just me.

I don't think my mother was able to express much physical affection. My oldest half-sister Nancy, the issue of my mother's first marriage to Tom McDonough who also died young, was 16 at the time of our mother's death. She remembered our mother as being very "reserved," and given to reading a lot, mostly popular magazines. Perhaps I was so fat because she nurtured me with food.

The explanation for our mother's reserve was clear enough. Her mother, Annie, was an accomplished woman in some respects. She drove her own automobile at a time when it was unusual for a woman to do so and she seems to have had some success in the real estate business before things went south. She was also an alcoholic. Many times, I'm told, our mother came home from school to find her mother drunk and had to pour the remaining liquor down the sink. At least twice Annie was incarcerated in the Park Sanitarium off Masonic Avenue to dry out. I suppose my mother fit the definition of what would now be called "the adult child of an alcoholic."

And maybe that is why I acted out. It would have been on my fifth birthday, in October 1940 as I reconstruct things, that I hit Jackie McDonough in the head with a hammer. I had received a carpenter set containing child-sized tools. Friends of the family, the McDonough's, came with their son Jackie, a boy about my age, to celebrate the day. As Jackie approached, I laid him out with a hammer blow to the head. Jackie's mother said "He didn't mean it." My mother said "Yes he did." My mother was right. Once, later, my sister Maureen, 16 months older than me, and I each received colored baby chicks for Easter—a custom now blessedly in the past. I manhandled mine to death and then, jealous that my sister's was still alive, I stomped it.

In early December 1940 I had been ill and I was allowed to sleep at night in bed with my mother. She then become ill herself and I was removed to the living room couch. On the evening of December 2, my sisters Nancy and Maureen and my infant sister Sheila, who had been born the previous April, were in the kitchen. It was dinnertime and I was still on the living room couch, recuperating from whatever ailed me. My mother called my sister Maureen from the bedroom adjoining the kitchen, and as my sister entered the room our mother died. According to Maureen at the time, our mother's face was blue. I have since wondered whether I might have been the carrier of the bug that pushed her over the line. I had recently started kindergarten at Kate Kennedy School and been among other young children, excellent transmitters of disease as any teacher will attest. I never did see our mother again; we children were not allowed to attend the funeral. "Windy" Gallagher, I'm told, tried to hustle the church for a free burial gown, claiming that our mother was a member of the Third Order of St. Francis.

My father never slept in the 30th Street house after the night of our mother's death. He was superstitious about death. Certainly there were home-based deaths in his native Ireland and I have never heard of anyone there abandoning their homes on that account. (Frank McCourt's mother, however, did move at least twice to get away from the ghosts of her recently dead children.) Whatever the reason, my father sold the house and its contents, lock stock and barrel. Included in the sale were my mother's photo albums which would have contained any family pictures from earlier San Francisco generations. The mention of the loss of those pictures can still get a rise out of my sisters who credit my father with a lack of sensitivity. In truth, he was a product of his time and place, just as you and I are of ours.

His people were "tatie-hokers", peasant farm workers from Achill in West Mayo, Ireland, who made annual trips to Scotland to help harvest the crops, much as Mexican workers now come to the U.S. to work in the fields, or Oklahomans of an earlier generation followed the wheat combines. Perhaps they still do. My father came from a part of Ireland where the old ways still held sway. Much later he was visiting with us in Marin County 1969 and we watched the moon landing on television together. As the module was setting down, he confidently assured us that the astronauts would find the man in the moon. We never discussed the matter further. On a visit to Achill in the 1980s, I was reliably informed by a relative about the existence of fairies, and shown a fairy patch where the woman's husband—who was known to take more than a drop—was delayed on his homeward journey by a fairy who caused the pedals on his bicycle to revolve backward as he remained stationary in place.

It was a hard life at home in Ireland for my father's generation, as suggested by the need to travel to find work, and a hard life in Scotland as well, where the workday began at a 4 am dawn in the long days of the northern summer clime, and ended only with the twilight, many long hours later.

It was a life that bred practical traits without much room for sentimentality about such things as photographs. When I was twelve, my father asked me if I was still interested in that Christmas present foolishness.

By his mid-twenties, my father was a gaffer, or working foreman, whose job it was to arrange for the transport of the squad to Scotland; bargain with the contracting farmers for a price; and see to the housing of his charges. It was a position of trust, usually held by men in their fifties, suggesting that he had a high level of responsibility.

In 1929, he came to the U.S., thinking he could better his lot, and arrived just before the Great Depression hit. Great timing. Originally, he went to Cleveland to where many Achill people had immigrated, and then he came on to San Francisco at the urging of his sister, Bridgie, who feared he was getting too involved with other Achill men in the Prohibition Era bootlegging industry there. First he worked out of Murray and Reidy's South of Market hiring hall which placed agricultural workers in valley farms. For a time he was an itinerant valley farm worker like those featured in John Steinbeck's pre-Okie era novel *Of Mice and Men.*

Then he returned to San Francisco where he worked as a "cowboy" for Good Brother's Dairy in Glen Park, keeping the dairy cattle out of the kitchen gardens of householders on Diamond Heights. My father was of an entrepreneurial bent and soon he converted an automobile, a Barley 6, into a truck, and started delivering milk on his own, to people whose custom he had solicited. After he met and married my mother, he gave up the milk business and took over the tea delivery route that had belonged to my mother's first husband. (Tom McDonough had a British warrant out for him, according to family lore, because of his involvement in the "Troubles." He is supposed to have kept all his cash in a money belt on his person so he would be ready to depart at a moment's notice.) The tea route evolved into my father's own butter and egg delivery business with which he provided fresh goods, bought from Petaluma and the Majoria Creamery on Haight Street, largely to the city's Irish housewives.

Some of my experiences must have been less melancholy than those related. Some of it was plain mischief. It was during this period that I tried to learn how to drive an automobile. We had a '37 or '38 blue Ford sedan. One of its features was a small red button light on the dashboard which was illuminated when the ignition was engaged by a floor pedal. I asked my father how to start the auto and he demonstrated by letting me push the red light on the dashboard. I did it and, sure enough, the bulb lighted up, and the engine started. A few days later, when there was no one else around, I tried to start the car myself by pushing on the light button; it didn't work of course. My first lesson in adult duplicity.

Once, my sister Nancy gave me 50 cents to go to the "new store" at Day Street to buy a can of peas. Instead, I went down to Church Street with Benny from Laidley Street where we bought a water gun.

Unable to find a water source, we urinated in a can to obtain ammunition. When I returned home, sans peas and with a water gun, Maureen was dispatched to return the gun for the money, which she did, and I locked myself in the bathroom. I either wouldn't, or couldn't, unlock the door, and my father had to dismantle it when he came home to get me out.

In the days before supermarkets, corner groceries could not keep fresh vegetables and dairy products because of the loss through spoilage. This gave rise to the home delivery businesses and the presence in the city's neighborhoods of trucks filled with vegetables; butter and eggs; fish; and other perishable goods, to be sold directly to housewives at their door. The last vestige of this industry was the milk delivery man who has now passed for the most part into history.

I still run into San Franciscans of a certain age who remember as children the arrival of my father, the "egg man," in their neighborhoods. In those quieter days his arrival constituted an event, at least from a child's perspective. He did pretty well on his route. He later told me that he made enough before the war to pay double house payments on the mortgage on the 30th Street house.

He served another function in the Irish community as well. In those days, before the widespread proliferation of automobiles, people were pretty much restricted to their own neighborhoods. He moved among the districts as sort of a mobile news agency, learning of the latest local news which he transmitted to his Irish housewife customers elsewhere. For this he was paid with more news or, sometimes, his customers would ply him with a drink to prime the news pump, and to distract him from their mounting unpaid balances.

He reveled in this activity though it often slowed him down on his job. One day I sat waiting in the car for him to make a delivery. I must have four or five at the time and to my mind he had been gone for too long. To punish him, I removed the pages of the small binder in which he kept his accounts and threw them out the car's window. When he returned he had to round up the pages which had by then been dispersed by the wind. He was angry with me, and I remember that my behavior was a subject of discussion when I got home. But he didn't hit me. It seems I was the only violent one in the family.

When the war came, and gasoline was rationed, he had to suspend operations for the duration. He went to work first as a bus driver and later as a warehouseman at the Marine building at 100 Harrison Street. He resumed his route after the war and held on for a few years, but the growth of supermarkets—which by now were able to refrigerate perishable foods—finally ended his business. That and unsustainable accounts receivable and the changing social climate in the city.

As I read the growing-up stories of others, alternately brutalized or abandoned by cruel fathers, I am thankful for the father I had. "Jimmy" Mullen was a minstrel boy. His life's delight was to hold forth *a capella* at social events with one of the countless Irish ballads in his truly immense repertoire. In the pre-tv, even pre-radio, world from which he came, people had to make their own entertainment. Aunt Bridgie told me that first- class passengers on the ship bringing her to the U.S. used to come down into steerage to watch the entertainment put on by the Irish immigrants. At San Francisco house parties, they would literally roll back the rugs and dance the sets and stack-o-barley, or highland fling, shouting and stamping their feet, to the accompaniment of Cousin Eddie Gallagher on the fiddle. Some would give recitations and Jimmy Mullen would hold forth with well-received renditions of "Come back Paddy Riley to Bally James Duff", or "The Garden where the Praties Grow," or maybe "Kevin Barry," among a host of others.

As a child I was embarrassed in front of my friends by his different accent, working-man's attire, and old fashioned country ways. A product of his time and place, he did not dispense physical affection easily but, unlike many others, he always saw to our creature needs. Even after his little business failed and he took work as a janitor at the age of 49, you could be sure that after a week on the job, the boss would turn over the keys to him. He was highly responsible.

Drink had a place in his life, although as far as I was able to see it did not affect his ability to function. As a young man, he took the Pioneers' Pledge to abstain from alcohol. As far as I know, he didn't drink anymore before our mother's death.

When his life became more difficult in later years, he was given to take drop. But he was never mean and cruel to us and he always discharged his obligations. He rejoined the Pioneers in his later years and drank no more. He did the best he could and that was better than most in his situation.

We didn't last long at Aunt Bridgie's. My father later said that "Bridgie wouldn't have you." Her version was that he wouldn't take responsibility for our discipline. In any case we soon moved out, and came under the influence of someone who had no problem at all taking responsibility for our discipline.

2 – 22nd Street

The way John Smith tells it, I mounted the stairs to 3919 22nd Street that summer day in 1941 and announced for all to hear "My name is Kevin Mullen and I am five years old." A brave entrance for a little guy—much braver than I ever really felt at the time, I'm sure. After leaving Bridgie's, we were taken in by Rose Smith to her boarding house- cum-foster home on 22nd Street. You would have to say that Rose Smith raised me, for that is where I lived most of the time, off-and-on, until my departure at 18 to join the army.

Rose Smith was a widow with five children of her own, Charles, Brendan, Emmett, John and Rosemary. She and her husband, Charles, had been well fixed in the 20s but they lost the hotel they owned in the Depression and later Charles died. Rose was left with five growing children of her own and no marketable skills. She did know about children, however, and she began "to take in kids," at first on her own and then through Catholic Social Services. First were the Logans, Jack Bill, and Leonard, whose mother had died and whose father couldn't care for them. We were next in 1941, Nancy, Maureen, Sheila and I.

Shortly before then, Rose had moved with her brood from their place on the 3800 block of 22nd Street to 3919, the house of Ellen Tully, an aging widow whose only son had died. Mrs. Tully was to be part of our life for the next two decades which she spent cautioning my sister Sheila not to marry an Englishman, a Protestant or a divorced man.

My first impressions there were of being stripped of all my mobile equipment. I had a solid-tired two-wheeled bike which my father had brought home to me from the family of another little boy who died. I think it was the very day we arrived that Rosemary, who was three or four years older than me, broke the chain by catching the skirt of her dress in it. The bike sat unfixed in the basement until we moved out years later. A few days later, John, a couple of years older than Rosemary, made my *Radio Flyer* wagon useless by destroying the steering mechanism when he ran it into a water faucet jutting from the side of the apartment building down the street. The collective adult judgment was that wheeled vehicles had no place on a steep hill anyway. So I spent the rest of my childhood on foot.

That fall, I entered the first grade St Philip's Grammar School in Noe Valley which I attended for the next six years. It was there I had what one could call a seminal experience, one that greatly influenced the rest of my life. I remember the room still in my mind's eye. It was a sunny one-storied building adjacent to the multi-storied main building which today looks much the same. It was in that room, very early in the school year, that we were handed Capitol Readers, blue bound books with an image of the nation's capitol embossed on the front cover. The first page read:

"I saw a dog.
His name is Happy.

Happy wants to run.
Happy wants to jump.
Happy wants to play."

We were soon on to the next page which included more sophisticated words like "mother" and "father" and told the story of "Puff, the kitten." "I've got it," I thought to myself. I now knew how to read. Since that day, reading has been a central factor in my life. Some have told me that reading is not a hobby or an occupation, but merely a pastime—just another escape from reality. I don't know about all that, but I do know that I have gotten a lifetime of pleasure from reading, and what I have learned in that way has helped me in just about every other aspect of my life.

Other than for reading, I never did take to school all that much. Some of it was innate laziness, I suppose. I was able to get by without trying too hard, and most of the time that was enough. At the end of the third grade, I recall, I was unable to participate in the year-end Diocesan tests which certified our qualification to move on to the next grade because I was ill in bed. The verdict came home from school that the tests would be unnecessary because "Kevin was bright enough."

Figure 2-The Mullens. Kevin, Nancy (McDonough), Sheila, James, Maureen

When World War Two started, "the boys" joined up. For Charley it was the Navy and service on a sub-chaser in the Pacific. Jack was with the Army Air Corps in England, and Bill joined the Army invasion forces to Europe. Ours was one of the few houses to proudly display three blue stars on the flag in the front window.

To a kid the war was fun, if that's the word. In the early days, we huddled in the darkness behind drawn shades during air raid drills, straining to hear the sound of enemy planes. Once, a man was shot dead on the Golden Gate Bridge for failing to turn out his headlights during a blackout. We heard he had been signaling enemy subs. One thing I remember about those years was getting in many childish fights. They were harmless enough affairs but suggest to me now that I had a lot of anger in me.

Another impression which remains is that I was always embarrassed about my status at school. We would all get new dark blue uniform corduroy pants at the beginning of the school year. The other kids would get replacements during the year as theirs wore out. Not me, or anyone else in Mrs. Smith's ménage, I imagine. By years' end, while everyone else still had nice blue cords, mine were faded to grey and patched. That was a blow to my pride which I had in full measure.

I was ashamed to live in what amounted to a foster home. Whether by house *dictat* or personal shame, (probably the former) I knew that I could not bring friends to the house. Once, Rose Smith took the whole passel of us to the circus with complimentary tickets which originated I know not where. She was trying to do for us, I'm sure, but I was humiliated when she asked an usher in our hearing if there was a section set aside for "underprivileged children." I hated being pitied.

Not all was so grim. We had all the neighborhood distractions available to kids at the time. We would play one-foot-off–the-gutter on the "level" (Castro between 22nd and Alvarado). Then there was the double lot above 3919 that ran through to Alvarado where we would play pinky-on-a-bounce or have sod fights when the new weeds sprouted up in the spring. We had a neighborhood dog, Frisco, a mottled grey hound, which actually belonged to George Augustus and which to our mind was the toughest dog in town. I envied the Augustus boys. George would be allowed to go to school on rainy days sans raincoat and galoshes which to me was the height of boyhood freedom. They had a grandfather or great-grandfather, a very old man we called "Creampuff" who was supposed to have served in the Civil War. Possible, when you think about it.

For all the outward comradeship, I think I was always kind of an outsider. Sports were big in the neighborhood consciousness, and the Coast Baseball League was pre-eminent prior to the arrival of the major leagues and the ascendance of other professional sports. All the kids talked about it and had the batting averages of their heroes on the San Francisco Seals or Oakland Oaks down pat. Not wanting to be left out, I memorized everyone's batting averages as an intellectual enterprise, only to find that they changed the next day, and again the day after that. It was then I came to the realization that I really didn't much care about what their batting averages were, or anything much about professional sports.

We played basketball every time we got near a schoolyard court. At the top of the hill, though, there were no playgrounds or schoolyards, so most of the time we had to do with what we had. Our game was step-baseball played against the front steps of houses on the 2200 block of 22nd. The pink marbled stairs with the sharp corners were best.

There wasn't much reading material in the house on 22nd Street as I remember. There were a few big/little books left over from the older kids. And later I remember a book of Grimm's Fairytales and a child's book of illustrated bible stories. But for the most part I had to satisfy myself with the stories that appeared in the little weekly Catholic magazine we received in school and the "Treasury of

American Literature," an anthology of short fiction geared to each grade level. I remember my realization in about the 4th grade that I had read every story in my reader. I had read a book.

I went on to read the stories in the older kids' readers as well. But that was about the extent of it. I don't think there was time for much reading. There was school, then homework, and housework, after which we were allowed to play outside. In fact, we were forced to play outside, with orders not to come home until dark, because Rose Smith didn't want a bunch of kids cluttering up the house after school.

3 – The War

With "the boys" off at war, the Doherty orphans moved in: Ray, Arlene, and Emmett, and my education began in earnest under Ray's tutelage. I don't know what my life would have been had I not met him but it certainly have been less exciting, I'm sure. I mark the date of their arrival exactly in September, 1943, for they showed up the day I was hit by the ice truck in front of the Quinns' house on Castro Street. I had been swiping empty soft drink bottles from the rear porches of the apartments in Mrs. Kelly's building down the street, and turning them in for deposit at John Mullaney's store at the corner to buy candy and Royal Crown Colas.

I suppose I was on some kind of a caffeine or sugar high when I nipped a ride on a departing ice truck. The good places at the rear tailgate were all taken so I tried to climb up over the left rear fender. I lost my grip and fell under the wheel—and watched as my left knee was spit out, like a tennis ball, from under its rolling edge. An inch or so more and…

The way Ray tells it, he arrived that day from another foster home, down in the dumps from all the moving around. But his spirits were immediately revived when he saw all the excitement. (He likes excitement still.) There crowded into the foyer was the iceman in his leather jerkin, the mandatory collection of interested neighbors, and the emergency ambulance crew. In the middle of it all—the center of attention—was a kid pretty much like him. The only discordant note was struck by my sister, Maureen, who stood there bawling; and all along I'd thought she hated me. Anyway, Ray decided immediately that this was his kind of place, and his kind of kid.

His estimate of the kid dropped dramatically, however, when the ambulance attendant lowered my trousers to check the injury, and it was revealed to all assembled that the object of his admiration was wearing long-john underwear. Later Ray Bowers and Jimmy Lyons were added to the tribe, and other individuals came and went over the years.

Rose Smith was tough on kids, or so it seemed to me at the time. We liked it best when she went shopping downtown. It would take the better part of a day, during which we would be out from under the scrutiny of the all-seeing-eye. Women in those days dressed to go downtown, and we watched eagerly as she prepared to join the shopping wars. We knew the time was close when the hat with the veil went on. Then a final cup of strong tea to gather strength, on with the gloves, and off she went. Freedom.

Our one fear was that one of the girls would "tell." It seems now that our concerns on that account were overblown, at least as far as Rosemary was concerned. One time, while her mother was off shopping, Rosemary spied me out the kitchen window, burning candles on the back stairs' post (of which more later). I was sure my goose was cooked. But Rose returned and dinner went uneventfully that night; there was nothing the next day either—or ever.

I met Rosemary many years later, at Jack Logan's funeral, and asked her why she hadn't snitched me off. "Mother didn't want to hear anything from talebearers," Rosemary told me. "If she didn't see an offense or have other first hand knowledge, she didn't want to know about it." If only we had known. As it was, there was enough serious misconduct to keep the disciplinary machinery humming along nicely anyway.

It was at dinner time that the full scale of the household operation became apparent. Fifteen for an evening meal in the 12'x15' dining room was normal. Twenty was not uncommon. The kids did all the non-cooking chores, and to this day I can peel potatoes and hand wash dishes faster than anyone who didn't grow up in that house.

Figure 3-Rose Smith and Kids. Ray Doherty at left.

Still there was always an extra place at the table. During the war it was the custom—when every family had someone in the service—to invite servicemen for dinner. How he arrived there I don't know, but I remember one soldier from Texas who wouldn't eat an artichoke because he thought it was a cactus. One military guest I do remember. A Marine cousin from Cleveland, Eddy Gallagher, came through San Francisco on his way back from one of the landings in the South Pacific and hooked up with my father. There was some later talk, as I recall, that he may have been shell-shocked. Anyway, I attached myself to him like a limpet. He gave me a Marine Corps tee shirt which I wore through subsequent washings until the emblem, and later the shirt itself disappeared into oblivion. He gave me a fifty cent piece when he returned to Cleveland and I remember feeling terrible at the time.

It was at holiday meals, though, that the dining operation received its severest test. In addition to the regular household, there would be Henry and Marie Columbo from Burlingame. Marie's sister Anna Deighan would come over from Seacliff where she worked as a maid. The Bowens would come up from 23rd Street, and maybe the Arrigonis from lower on 22nd. John Lacoste, the butcher from the Eureka Market, would carve the bird, all the while making mildly irreverent comparisons between the tail end of the turkey and the "Pope's nose." Johnny Matthews, Rose Smith's god-father, often made the scene, with his fiddle and always ready joke. Johnny was a bit of a mystery man. The kids weren't brought in on the details but it seems that he didn't need to work, having had something to do with adult beverages during the Prohibition years. He moved into the house for a time as well.

Because of the crowd at holiday meals, the kids had to sit in the kitchen, with one ear cocked to what was going on at the main table. There would be enough wine to stimulate spirited conversation among the adults, but that was the extent of it; ours was a respectable house. Before each large dinner, Rose Smith would establish the ground rules for discussion. To avoid disruptive disputes, certain subjects would be declared taboo. There would be no talk, she would insist, about Ireland, the Catholic Church, or politics. "Of course," my father later told me, "that's all anyone wanted to talk about," so the ground rules soon went out the window, often dispatched on their way by Rose herself.

My father—because of his status as a small businessman—leaned toward the Republican Party. Still, my sense is that the prevailing political sentiment in the neighborhood was pro-Roosevelt. Even as elementary school children during the 1944 presidential election, we just *knew* that if Dewey was elected, he was going to order school on Saturdays. Roosevelt's death, like that of Kennedy's assassination and the 9/11 terror attack, is one of those events which everyone who was alive at the time will remember forever. I was in the hallway of St. Philip's school for some reason; it was after classes let out for the day when the word was received of the President's death. I was wearing my badly faded Marine Corps tee shirt.

We learned of the war's end a few months later from the off-hour tolling of St. Philip's church bells. It was evening and neighbors took the pots off their stoves and headed for 3919 to celebrate. Rose Smith was a force in the neighborhood, not just the house. From a kid's point of view, the adult celebration was a much needed respite from adult supervision. Ray and I ranged unfettered through the neighborhood that night, and while older miscreants rioted on Market Street we conducted physics experiments with Castro Street busses by jamming potatoes up their exhaust pipes to stall them out.

It was much the same on Halloween. In that time and place, Halloween was the province of 10 to 12 year old boys who prowled the night-time neighborhood looking for trouble. It was too serious a business to leave to the five year-old goblins who now come around on Halloween, their parents waiting at the end of the driveway as they ring the bell. Trick or treat must have just been coming into vogue because half the houses didn't know what we were talking about when we made our demands. With no candy laid in, they would good-naturedly try to find some sweets to pay the extortion. And just as well for in those days, if there was no treat, there was a real trick. John Mullaney would put glycerin on his store windows to foil our attempts to wax them. We would find others, though, who lacked his foresight. It was like a low-grade guerilla conflict between prepubescent boys and certain householders who took delight in trying to scare the bejesus out of us.

The War over, "the boys" came home. I remember a uniformed Jack Logan getting off the bus on Castro, the round blue patch with gold wings of the Air Corps emblazoned on his left sleeve. Emmett left the seminary, and the house was fuller than ever. Charley Smith married Anna Rose Lacoste (from the 3800 block of 22nd) that year, and went into the shoe business where he made a great success. Ray and I drained the glasses at their reception, and he got so sick I had to do his paper route the next day.

Jack Logan went to college on the G.I. bill—the first one we knew to aspire to a higher secular education. And Bill went "on the cops" with his friend Bill Murphy from down on 23rd Street. The night before Bill Logan was sworn in, Rose Smith sewed a Sacred Heart medallion into the inner left breast of his police blouse. Bill later married Marcella, Rose Smith's niece from Chicago.

I have often wondered what my life would have been like if Ray had not come on the scene. Since my arrival at five years old I had called Rose Smith "Mommy Smith" as I had been instructed when I moved in. Ray made it clear to me that I should not call her that because she was not my mother. Thereafter, I never again addressed the woman by any name. Until I finally left her domain at the age of 18, I would merely address her by talking to her without using her name. I learned much at Ray's side. I still do.

At night, there would be a half hour or so of radio time allowed. My favorites were Red Ryder, The Lone Ranger, and the Cisco Kid. One of the big disappointments of my young life—and a lesson in the superiority of imagination over reality—came years later when first I saw the Lone Ranger on a television show. I was well past the fan stage by then but still I was disappointed that the image of the man and his horse could not measure up to the picture I had formed in my mind, including as it did, fire spurting from Silver's nostrils.

I'd have to say that my sisters and I weren't close. On one level our membership in the pack of kids in Smith's house blurred nuclear familial lines but on another level our sibling connection was clear. Our father would take us together most Sundays to a park, or the beach, or to visit some of his friends. I formed the opinion that my sisters didn't like me much. Once, Sheila flung a brass figure of a griffin at me, striking me in the head. Perhaps—and I suspect this was so—she was harboring the same sort of demons that prompted me to stomp the baby chick and hit Jackie McDonough in the head with a hammer.

It probably had something to do with not getting enough attention. I remember being present at a school recital where we all sat cross-legged on the floor while other students played the piano and other instruments. I was either bored or feeling neglected and as one girl walked by me on her way to the piano, I shot my leg out, tripping her. I denied any hostile intent to the nun and to Mrs. Smith when she received the note from the sister. I can admit it now. I did have hostile intent.

Maureen seems to have delighted in snitching me off when I had done something wrong. Once she held it over my head for what seemed like months that I had pulled up Donna's dress and pulled down her pants. (I was fascinated, I think, that the dress and the pants were made of the same flowered cotton material. There were probably some nascent sexual stirrings as well.) Anyway I was relieved when my sister finally snitched me off and I received the punishment due such crimes, a lashing by Rose Smith with a cat-o-nine tails, a section of razor strop with its end cut into thin, two inch long strips. (Someone had taken the trouble to intentionally fabricate a device designed to inflict the maximum amount of stinging pain with the least effort. Hmm.)

One thing I noticed as a child was that my father favored the girls, first Maureen, then later Sheila as she came along. I suppose it came from some old-country belief that boys should be tough. In any event, he always had them on his lap and clearly seemed to enjoy their company more than mine. There were advantages to being a boy, I suppose. I was given first shot at the shotgun seat in the car. And when it came to his dying 40 years later it was to me my father turned to supervise his departure.

4 - Benicia

In the summer of 1946, Rose Smith took a war-delayed summer-long visit to her family in Ireland and the Mullen kids were shipped off to St. Catherine's Academy, actually a Dominican run quasi-orphanage/day school in Benicia (where the Solano Shopping Center now stands.) As far as I know, there was no intention that we would return to the Smith house after her vacation. I think there was a crowding problem, what with Rose's son Emmett out of Maryknoll Seminary and the "boys" back from the war.

In Benicia we lived in dormitories supervised by Dominican nuns, the same folks who gave us the Spanish Inquisition. That's perhaps carrying the comparison too far. Some of the nuns were kindlier than others. I specifically remember a Sister Genevieve, though, a heavy red-headed freckled woman who was not. During that summer we would be taken down to the water's edge occasionally to "swim" in the cold and, to me, dirty Bay. Once we went to Conception Arguello's grave on a hill behind the orphanage. There were Sunday visits by our father. The food was rotten there but all-in-all it could have been a lot worse.

People then didn't seem to consider that adult actions could cause psychic damage to their children, as evidenced by Sheila's experience at St. Catherine's. She was six months old when our mother died, and she came to Rose Smith's not long after her first birthday. Her first conscious memories, she says, are of being physically nurtured by Rose. (Rose Smith may have been tough on kids but she loved babies.) As Sheila remembers it, she felt warm and secure in Rose's embrace during her years leading up to 1946. Then, with no warning, she was bundled up and off to a strange institution under the supervision of impersonal nuns. It had to have been psychologically wrenching. (It's much like the practice of the upper classes at the time, British and American, who sent their sons off to boarding schools in much the same way, causing all sorts of recorded psychic damage.) All three of us were sent there. I was older than Sheila, though, and had by then, I imagine, already formed the shell with which I greeted the world.

One humiliating experience stands out. I guess I wasn't the best-behaved boy and I suppose my sisters must have had some problems as well, for on one occasion in the dining hall at lunch time, one nun announced to the assembled children that the Mullen family was no good. I remember explicitly that she included the entire family in her charge. I suspect this reinforced my own feelings of inadequacy because I remember my impotent rage to which I was unable to give voice, partly because I may have believed that what she said was true.

I checked this out later with my older sisters and they confirmed my reading. There were two status tiers at Rose Smith's house, her kids, and everyone else. It's natural enough for a woman, no matter how generous she might be, to favor her own over others. That's the way I felt treated, and my sisters did too—that somehow we were flawed in some way, that we just didn't measure up. Maybe it was something in us; it's not the sort of feeling that goes away easily. It can drive one to excellence, or to despair. Self esteem is what they call it.

At 11, I was the oldest boy at St. Catherines. No boys older than 10 were permitted in residence. This status gave me a certain freedom not allowed to the other boys. I was often sent to town on a battered bicycle on a host of small errands, like picking up the fish each week for the Friday meal. I was thus able to explore the back streets of the then moribund (but no longer) town of Benicia.

I expect the age limit had something to do with the nuns not wanting to deal with pubescent boys, and probably with good reason as things turned out. It was at Benicia that my romantic life blossomed. Not sex, romance. As the oldest boy, I was the principle subject upon which the blossoming girls could work out their romantic fantasies. (It's a condition perhaps analogous to retirement homes where women greatly outnumber men and the few men present are in demand as romantic partners.) There was a lot of kissing, as I recall but that was it. I liked it. Then it stopped as soon as it started. I think that had something to do with the resumption of the school year and the availability of a larger number of age-appropriate male day students.

It was there I got another lesson about the essential injustice of the world. At St. Catherine's, I was the senior altar boy, having received my basic training earlier at St. Philip's. Indeed, I was the boy who trained the younger boys in the mysteries of the liturgical rites. It was announced one day that the Archbishop was coming, and the entire establishment was thrown into a frenzy of preparation for his visit. Windows were washed; the foliage on the grounds was trimmed; and floors were scrubbed where the holy man would never set foot. The highpoint of the bishop's visit was to be the high mass at which he would preside.

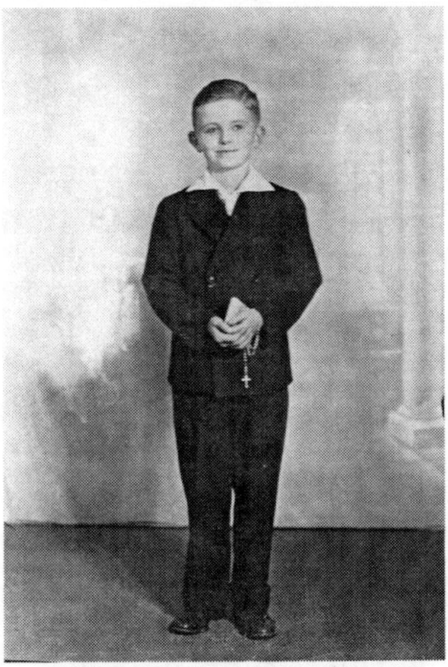

Figure 4-The Altar Boy

As senior man, I was sure I had a lock on being the principal server at the mass. Consider my dismay when I was told that I would be passed over in favor of two of my shorter acolytes who were of matched height. My sense of fairness was outraged at St. Catherine's, and I harbored enmity against those who had treated my so shabbily for years. I don't think it would have helped for me to have understood then that liturgical services have a distinct theatrical dimension to them, and when putting on a show, it's best if the members of the corps are pretty much the same height.

For some reason, I became seriously "run down." I was told I was suffering from malnutrition. Perhaps it had something to do with my own "weak chest" but I don't recall having any bronchial attacks at that time. The first sign of the condition was that I started losing fights with other boys I thought I should have won. I just didn't have the strength. This last may have been a blessing in disguise, for I had to learn, earlier than some, that physical violence with one's peers is not always the best default position when one is confronted with petty frustrations. It can help a fellow develop his personality.

I remember staying for a while in St. Catherine's infirmary where I read Robert Louis Stevenson's *Kidnapped.* Then I was sent back to Rose Smith to recuperate while my sisters remained. At Smith's I was ensconced on a day-bed in the alcove of the dining room facing out on the back yard. I stayed there for some time, night and day, recuperating, even as members of the household ate their meals around me. I was finally built-up enough to return to school at St. Philips but I don't think I fully recovered physically until I was in the army. I stayed at Smith's for the next few years while my sisters were moved to the Dominican boarding school at St. James on Guerrero Street.

Sometime in 1947, things began to get weird. Ray didn't want to play step baseball anymore, or "pinky on a bounce." He was satisfied to hang around down on 24th Street, mooning over Cathy Goolden. It's not that I didn't know about romance. I had had my romantic interlude at St. Catherine's, and once before been in love myself, with Kay of the golden curls. Sometime earlier, I had the most sublime moment in my pre-teen life when I beat up Raul Aguilar on the last day of school in St. Philip's school yard for the hand of Kay, while Kay and her friend Betty looked discreetly on.

Actually, I don't know for sure what Kay thought about it all because we never discussed the matter. (Bob Bassett told me later that every boy in the class was as smitten with her as I.) There was a social justice dimension to the conflict, anyway. Raul had a nickel plated bike, and I had none; and the cosmic balance of justice required an adjustment. We can pass over my fight with Steve Spina in the vacant lot at 23rd and Diamond which I started, over nothing, and he finished.

But I didn't learn the desperation of real eye-gouging, ear-biting, head-banging, no-holds-barred combat until I mentioned to Ray, innocently enough, that Cathy Goolden and John Shea would make a fine looking couple together. In the ensuing fight he disabused me of that notion. But not without a cost. He is two years older than I am and so tended to come out on top during our earlier childhood brawls. But he would be the first to tell you that, due to pride, or stubborn contrariness, or whatever, I refused to give in, to quit, to "say uncle." He would sometimes give up himself, he says, for fear of doing real damage me. Always smarter than I was in such matters, he, when I got older and we became more equal in size, decided that we would no longer decide these issues by brute force but would instead resolve them through negotiation. Dope that I am, I went along with his plan.

In 1948 we moved away from Noe Valley, and from our childhood as well—to the Sunset, the first step in the now familiar migration of San Franciscans of that generation to suburbia. From the comparative safety of adulthood, and with the help of welcome insights from Ray, I can now understand why Rose Smith was so strict with us. If she had let down her guard for a moment, she would have been overrun by the horde of half-tamed little barbarians in her charge. It is central to an understanding of juvenile crime these days that broken families contribute greatly to the problems of society. Through Rose Smith's efforts, I'm sure, San Francisco was spared more serious delinquency than that which did occur.

5 – 10th Avenue

In 1948, the entire household moved from 3919 22nd Street to 1454 Tenth Avenue where we occupied both of the flats, the downstairs of which served as sort of men's dormitory. Emmett Smith had the back bedroom. For a time Tom Carroll, an old friend from Rose's native County Cavan, who had been blinded in a railroad explosion as a young man, had the other bedroom. Jimmy Lyons, one of the foster kids, had a bed in the little kitchen. Jack Logan had the adjoining breakfast nook and John Smith and Bill Logan shared what would have been the dining room. I slept in what was the living room with a rotating group of others, two at a time.

For one period it was me, Leonard Logan and Ray Doherty. At another time, it was me, my father and Jimmy Duffy, an 82 year old man who stood up most of the night trying to urinate into a chamber pot. (Let those who yearn for the good old days consider what modern prostate procedures could have done for Jimmy Duffy.) The girls and Mrs. Tully were disposed around upstairs. At some point my sisters returned to the household and later Mrs. Bowen, the elderly lady from the parties on 22nd Street, joined the ménage. (Rose worked both ends of the street, foster children and elders. When the social service folks came to inspect for the kids, the elders had to disappear, and I remember being told to make myself scarce when people came to check on the oldsters.)

Tom Carroll, the blind man, contributed much to my early understanding of the city beyond our own neighborhood. Tom sold brooms door-to-door around town and did very well for himself. Deeply religious, he would attend daily mass to which I lent my arm as a guide. I would also take him around town to attend the annual summer novenas. It was while doing this that I got my first inkling that there was a San Francisco beyond the grim, treeless Mission or fog-bound Inner Sunset.

One evening I escorted him by Muni bus to attend a novena at St. Peter and Paul's, I think, in North Beach. It was one of those clear warm summer evenings and the sky was pink with clouds when we stepped off the Stockton Street bus at Columbus into a different world. The produce was piled in front of the stores and the Italians bustled about in good numbers, shouting back and forth to each other. It was if I had been transported to a Mediterranean village. The place has much the same effect on me even today.

Tom Carroll finally had to go. One night when Rose Smith was out, Tom brought home a male friend who he had met at The Stein, a saloon at 9th and Irving. They drank further and then the friend decided he was going to help Tom get into bed. The fight was on and was resolved only when Emmett Smith confronted the guy with Bill Logan's .45 caliber pistol. Tom's right hand was a twisted three-fingered claw from the same railroad explosion. He must have acquitted himself pretty well in the fight, though, because the lumbering giant being escorted down the hall at gunpoint was pretty well bloodied up. Tom disappeared the next day and I never saw or heard of him after that.

I suppose we moved because the sharp incline from Castro Street up to 3919 was becoming too steep for Rose Smith to climb easily as she got older. There was another reason, I suspect, as well. The town was changing and it was thought that the Mission District was changing more. It was a time when there was a great deal of concern about post-war juvenile crime. I remember first hearing the term latch-key kid, and learning what the term meant, at 3919.

My sense is that Rose wanted to get the younger boys, Ray and I, away from the bad influences we would be more likely to encounter there than in the Sunset. Perhaps her concerns were well placed. Most of the kids from around there turned out OK as far as I know with a couple of notable exceptions. A guy we called "Rabbit" who lived up the street on 22nd was one of the five shot (two died) by Robert Ranson at the Butchers' Ball in Civic Center in 1952. That was the last Butcher's Ball, I think, another sign of the changing times. It was customary for all kinds of organizations to host annual balls in large auditoriums, but by the 1950s the fights which tended to break out there put an end to them. It was the same thing with the regular benefit dances held in Larkspur by the Volunteer Fire Department since before the War and which attracted large numbers of young people from the city. By the 1950s they had to be discontinued because of all the fighting. For some reason, our immediate predecessors got along without a lot of public fist-fighting.

And Bobby Halligan, from over on Alvarado Street, who we used to hang with, was arrested and convicted of a robbery/murder at Siri's Market in 1957. (I sold him his first gun, a bb pistol for fifty cents. I spent it all on candy—that was a lot of candy in that economy—and was soon informed by my stomach that more isn't necessarily better when it comes to good things.) Bobby had always been a bit wilder than the rest of us and even earlier we knew he was given to fits of ungovernable rage. On one earlier occasion, while walking home from school for lunch from St. Philips, Bobby stuck my sister Maureen in the behind with the pointed end of a compass. Maureen duly reported the offense to Rose Smith who told her to go tell Mrs. Halligan. Maureen marched over to Alvarado Street and rang the doorbell to the Halligan house. Her bad luck. Bobby answered the door and threw her down the stairs. Maureen returned and reported the compounded crime to Rose Smith who, by this time, had exhausted her allotment of justice on that particular case, so there the matter remained.

Though we lived in the Sunset, I continued at St. Philips until such time as I could be accepted in St. Anne's. When I think about today's parents who won't let their children out of their sight, I think of the lengthy bus and street-car trip I took alone back and forth across the city to school daily, sometimes in the dark of early night. Finally I was admitted to St. Anne's where I met friends, some of whom I remain in regular contact with to this day.

It was here that I got my first job, delivering copies of the *San Francisco News* under the supervision of Al Grangoff, legendary circulation boss. My route (GG 11) ran up 9th Avenue from Judah to Noriega and back down 10th including side streets. I don't know how long I kept the route but as I think about it in the end I got fired for some reason which now escapes my memory. I do remember that I figured out a way to embezzle from myself so that I could buy candy. The result was that in many months I showed no profit at all.

St. Anne's was OK. About this time, based on my experiences at St. Catherine's and some at St. Anne's I began to doubt the basic Christianity of some of the nuns. I remember being warned off several occasions of sin. One was Rudy's, a little notions store and circulating library on Judah between 9th and 10th. It was the ideal place for kids to hang out. In addition to what could be called adult magazines, the store had comic books and candy as well as other gimcracks which would appeal to kids.

Rudy was a little balding man who always wore a smock and lived in the back of the store. Intimations that there was more to his life than appeared on the surface became apparent when a Jane Russell-type brunette showed up one day to share his backroom and help out at the store. (Many years later, in the 1980s, I ran into Rudy, who then had to have been 90, on the 5th floor of the Hall of Justice. He appeared lost so I introduced myself to him as one of his customers from the 1940s and offered to direct him to where he wanted to go. He blushingly told me that he was looking for the 6th floor [the city prison floor] because he knew some 'young women' up there. It seems that Rudy was still hobnobbing with the girls, even at that advanced age.)

Less defensible was the nuns' caution to stay away from Herman Theriault and Charlie Strom. The only reason we could figure out was that their mothers were divorced single-parents, trying to raise their children alone. I'm sure that the nuns had our best interest at heart but that can't have been easy on Herman and Charlie. (As a matter of fact, I later got to know Herman's mother, Mrs. T, very well when she provided a sanctuary for the "lost boys" of the neighborhood.)

I always did OK in school if I gave it any effort at all. The problem was that much of the time I didn't give it much effort. In the 8th grade I was relegated to the rows at the left rear of the room which the discipline problems shared with the slow learners. I suppose I was there for some kind of disciplinary problem. One day I was throwing pencils at Bobby Allen whose desk was in the window row. He was throwing them back at me. One pencil bypassed him and went out the window, almost hitting a priest who was walking by. He came to the classroom and, after somehow identifying the culprits, took us to the priest house where he heard our confession. I imagine I had some sense of proportionality even then because I remember thinking that throwing pencils was hardly a confession-level offense.

One day, Sister Cyril McDonald—a good woman and one of the nuns who I remember fondly—kept me after school. (I didn't know it at the time but her police officer father had been murdered in the line of duty at the Crystal Palace Market on 8th Street in the 1930s.) In an effort to influence my behavior for the good, Sister Cyril asked me whether I didn't want to grow up and have a decent family. To accomplish that, she told me, I would have to succeed in school. A comic-strip light bulb went off above my head. The nuns were always trolling in those days for likely candidates—those with the academic chops—to steer them to the seminary. I guess I had been listening to the sales pitches because in answer to the good nun's question I said "No." "Then what do you want," she said? "I want to be a priest," I replied.

Big mistake. Sister hooked right into it and when my father heard about it I was stuck. Having a priest in an Irish family at that time was a feather in the familial cap. There was no going back. I moved, at first willingly, into a new realm, both with teachers and my fellow students. I started attending mass daily. My religious observance, as I look back on it, was obsessive at that period. I was moved over to the "good row" by the window, just behind John Ring and Ron Lambers, both of whom went on to be ordained priests. My grades soared into the mid-90s when I began to apply myself—but not quite as high as those of John and Ron who doubtless had a better foundation, having paid attention to the teachers in earlier years. I changed in the eyes of my fellow students as well. I remember once they picked me to umpire a softball game, about which I probably knew less than most, on the grounds that as a prospective seminarian I would be fair to a fault.

I have sometimes felt bad about tricking Sister Cyril that way because she was a genuinely good woman. I could excuse myself by claiming that I was encouraged down that false path by the vocational suggestions I and my classmates had received from the nuns. On long reflection, however, I thank Sister Cyril for encouraging my "vocation" and have concluded that my stay at the seminary, though I went there flying under false colors, was a positive experience, and one whose memories I treasure to this day. In September 1949, I entered St. Joseph's Minor Seminary at Mountain View. At the entry physical exam I learned that I was 5′1″ tall and weighed 100 lbs.

6 – St. Joseph's

The first rule we learned of at St. Joseph's was that you never, ever, entered another student's room. It was an absolute rule. Violate it and you would be immediately dismissed. Like most 13 year-olds I internalized the rule and never entered another's room. Neither did I question the reason for the rule at the time. It was one of those mysterious adult proscriptions that didn't have, or need to have, any rational explanation.

I was ill-suited, as I soon found out, for the object of a seminary education, even though I treasure the experience. Our lives are enriched by the variety of experiences we have, and, for me, the seminary experience in its secular dimension was akin to the English public school experience or that of the live-in boarding prep schools in the East. After having spent a couple of years there, I was better able to relate to any number of books and movies, starting with *Tom Brown's School Days* and *Goodbye Mr. Chips,* and, more recently, *The Emperor's Club.* Even Joyce's *Portrait of the Artist as a Young Man.*

St. Joe's had all the similar types of traditions found in the classic boarding school experience. There was the communal life of school room and chapel presided over by learned men whose principal interest was our religious and intellectual development. There were the refectory meals at which upper classmen supervised tables while a student read from some approved, popular nonfiction books (I remember learning of Thor Hyerdahl's *Kon Tike* in this way.)

There were other traditions as well. There was the annual play, produced and performed by upperclassmen, in the tradition of boys' prep schools everywhere. (As I think about it here, the urge to perform on the stage in an all male setting seems to be universal. The Bohemian and Family clubs in San Francisco come to mind as do the Hasty Pudding Club at Harvard and its counterpart at Yale. No movie about a World War Two prison camp is complete without a scene of the inmates' play. A recurring image is that of some of the male actors dressed up as females. I wonder if something else is going on here. Later in the police department I became aware of the annual theatrical production put on by the detective bureau, which was challenged for importance only by the annual FBI/Detective Bureau Softball game. This is another area of male bonding that has eluded my interest.)

Figure 5-Songfest at St. Joes. "The kid" in suspenders.

Each Fall there was an immense bonfire, the pyre constructed over months with pieces of scrap lumber until the pile was maybe 20 by 20 by 20 foot in volume. One night in Autumn, probably Halloween as I think about it, the pile was set alight. I wonder if the good padres realized that they were party to the re-enactment of a pre-Christian pagan ritual. Probably so, for they were educated men and had a more sophisticated theological world view than had I at the time, or indeed now.

Then there were the intra-mural teams revolving around all the sports in season. I think we all played all sports and it was in this period that I played soccer and baseball and participated in track and field events for the first time. I could manage but I wasn't very good. (It was the only school setting in which I ever much cared about sports.) I can't claim that it was my lack of background, except for basketball, as contributing to my lack of success. That's because there was one classmate, a Mexican guy, who I think spent his youth working in the fields of San Joaquin Valley, and who was instantly the master of any sport that came to hand, no matter how unfamiliar he had been with it. On some level I learned the lesson that in life there was always someone who was going to best you, so it's best to play to your strengths. I don't know if that is the most adventurous life course to pursue, but it can prevent a lot of disappointment.

The academics were more demanding at the seminary than at other schools I had attended. But this presented no particular problem. I must have started reading books regularly by that time, though I have no recollection of any specific titles, because I remember missing the activity. During study periods, I would read the dictionary for want of secular reading fodder, which no doubt contributed to my acquisition of a fairly large recognition vocabulary.

It was at the seminary that I learned to swim. An insignificant event in the larger scheme of things but a subject which illuminates an aspect of my character which I have detected in other male members of my family: a sometimes excessive pride that can work in the end against self-interest, in my case almost fatally. In my late grammar school years and even after my first year at the seminary I attended St. Joseph's Camp in the summer. Run by Christian Brothers from St Mary's in Oakland, it was located at Moscow (between Monte Rio and Duncan's Mill on the Russian River). The later years there I earned my keep by working in the laundry.

The older kids divided themselves roughly into two groups. One group was comprised of what you could call the "naturalists.' They took to the river and surrounding terrain, fishing and exploring. The other group, of which I was mostly a member, were what I suppose you could call the "townies." We wore our Levis slung low and liked to go into Monte Rio acting tough to play the pinball machines.

There were grades of swimmers at the camp, from pollywog non-swimmers up through C, B and on to A, the most proficient. Since I was one of the high status older kids I was assumed by all to be a C swimmer at least, though I couldn't swim at all. And I didn't disabuse anyone of that fact. I had it figured out, though, how far I could jump from the dock and still keep my feet on the ground under me. One day, I jumped, and the waves from others who jumped after me pushed me out into deeper waters. I began to drown. I specifically remember thrashing around and trying to save myself. I also specifically remember not wanting to cry out because of pride. That damn pride.

Finally I gave up and lay half-suspended in the green sun-filtered river water as I slipped into unconsciousness. Fortunately, Ray Doherty was watching from the beach, saw my distress, jumped in the water and dragged me out. Without a doubt he saved my life and I don't think Brother Aloysius, our life guard, even knew what had occurred. (I later became a proficient swimmer and in my last year at camp, I regularly swam across the river to Rien's Beach.)

You might not think that there would be bullies at a seminary but there were. It was before I learned to swim and I was terrified of being dunked. There was this classmate from St. Lake City—of all places—who delighted in having his stooge, a guy from Oakland, dunk me when I ventured toward the deeper water in the pool. The guy from Oakland was a classic mesomorph, short but stout and with chiseled muscles. He had the advantage of non-swimmer me in the pool and never failed to exploit it. One night I got him alone on solid ground on the way to Vespers. He may have started it with his verbal taunts but when we were through, he didn't try to dunk me any more. I learned also that evening that appearances can sometimes be deceiving. Mesomorphs aren't necessarily well coordinated, or always as strong as they might look.

It was during my years at St. Joseph's that I experienced my sexual awakening. I suppose I would have been 13 or 14. I don't remember exactly, but once it occurred and I started thinking about girls in a different way, any thought of continuing with my "vocation" was out of the question. (I'm not going to talk about the specifics of my sex life except to say that I had one. The same thing goes for the particulars of my married life. I come from a generation and a group of people for which some subjects are off limits for public discussion.)

I can say that my sexual awakening was pretty mixed up. I don't know if my experience was any more confusing than that of others, but as tangled up as it was with my obsessive religiosity at the time, I went through a very troubling period. I remember strong erotic feelings when teachers would sometimes talk in great descriptive detail about young virgins who had suffered martyrdom rather than submit to defilement. In any event, full I suppose, of the sort of fearsome theology propounded to young Irish Catholics at the time, I came to believe that the devil was visiting me in my cell at night.

One night I went so far as to wake up my confessor who blessed my room. Much later I told a priestly friend—who incidentally had been a seminarian there at the same time—that I had in effect made a Faustian deal with the devil one dark and frightening night if only he would leave me alone about sexual things. The priest told me not to worry because the church had moved on in its thinking since then. Still I can't help but wonder sometimes if there is not something to the old ways, and that my day of reckoning is at hand. If not, and intellectually I think not, those were still terrible things they filled young impressionable heads with then, rendered humorously these days in Tee shirts with the legend: "I survived a Catholic education."

While all this was going on, I became aware of something which has much afflicted the church in recent years. The reason for the stricture about not entering another's room soon became evident. I began to discern a distinct homoerotic subtext in much that was going on in the seminary. It took the form of upperclassmen hitting—at least verbally—on the less developed members of the lower classes. One member of my class was singled out and assigned a female variation of his name by some upperclassmen, and he didn't like it one damn bit. They were jocular about it but my sense was that they were "kidding on the square." It was not everybody. I have talked to fellow seminarians in recent years, both from my year and members of upper classes. Some are aware of the phenomenon as having occurred, some not.

The faculty was death on it. That was for sure. One classmate of mine, given to talking about it in the abstract, just disappeared one day, supposedly after having propositioned another member of the class he had been talking about. I, myself, almost got caught up inadvertently in a situation. Another cardinal rule was that it was forbidden under pain of expulsion to swim nude in the pool, for reasons which by now should be obvious. There was a custom, though, during swimming season, to be the first, after classes let out, to rush to the pool compound, change into your suit, and "break the ice" by jumping into the pool. One day, I was leading the pack even as some others were gaining on me. To cut to the chase, I grabbed my suit and without putting it on, jumped into the deep end of the pool. Just at that moment, a priest entered the door at the far end of the pool area and spied me in the pool. He stood there for a moment, then turned around and left, no doubt figuring correctly that all was innocent, for within moments I was joined in the pool by a large number of other swimmers. I discreetly put on my suit, hiding behind the disturbed wave action caused by their arrival.

It is this experience that I bring to the current troubles of the church with pedophilia. I note that it is almost always committed with adolescent males, just about the age when young boys once—but no longer—were permitted to enter the seminary life. At the risk of getting over my depth in psychological analysis, I've come to the conclusion that the sexual development of these men was arrested just as it was blossoming in an all male environment which included a lot of teenaged boys. It's been said that the sexual impulse is like the smoke in a room on fire; if it can't find its way out the door it will escape through a window. I guess I believe that. I don't know whether the impulse is undifferentiated as some claim, but I believe that in a womanless setting, whether in prison, the navy or a seminary, the impulse will find a way to express itself.

In recent times, charges have been made that the church hierarchy has long known of the problem and ignored it by merely transferring errant priests to other positions where again children are vulnerable. My original thinking on this was that the church's way of looking at things was caught in a pre-psychology time warp. Psychologists seem to believe that by the time these proclivities are established they are more or less fixed. The basic tenet of the church is the absolute belief in redemption, no matter what the sin. Viewing the conduct as a sin permits the church to consider the matter closed as soon as a good confession is made. What psychology may consider as a condition, the church treats with as an individual event. More recent revelations suggest that the church had reason to know the damage that was being done, and some bishops, out of protection of the institution rather than the welfare of the faithful, acted despicably. All I know of my own knowledge, though, is that in the early 1950s at St. Joseph's Seminary, any such conduct was severely discouraged.

By the end of my second year at St. Joseph's I knew the priestly life was not for me. I told my father who discouraged me from leaving and I returned to start the third year. When my sister, Maureen, told Rose Smith that I didn't want to be there, Rose had my father go to get me. It was a chilly ride back to the city. I went back to Rose's house and entered St. Ignatius High School as a junior.

On several occasions in recent years I have been included in a series of dinners attended by former seminarians. Some, like me, "spoiled priests" in F. Scott Fitzgerald's term, dropped out along the way. Others were ordained priests before leaving. Still others remain under holy orders to this day. I have asked some of them why, in the 1960s and 70's, apparently for the first time in the history of the church, they had deserted the priesthood in such large numbers. For some, I'm sure, it was a crisis in faith. Others though, spoke of coming to inner-city parishes as educated young men in their 20's, wanting to minister to the social needs of parishioners, only to be restrained by older pastors, men from a different age, who required unquestioned obedience and seemed preoccupied with building funds and other non-ministerial considerations.

Whatever their reason for leaving the seminary or priesthood, I found these men in later life to be universally decent people. There are no captains of industry among them. Almost to a man they have spent their post-seminary working lives in one of the "helping" professions. I am proud to be counted among their number.

7 – Sex, Lies, and St. Ignatius

When I left the seminary, I entered at St. Ignatius High School, then in the old building at Turk and Stanyan streets. I ended up there by the sheerest chance. Coming from the household I did, it would be more likely that I would have gone to Sacred Heart or Riordan High like everyone else who grew up in the Smith house. I chose St. Ignatius because it was the only school I could remember where I knew somebody from grammar school. Or maybe the convenience of bus connections had something to do with it.

Back in Rose Smith's house, I went to work part-time, after school and on Saturdays, as a stock boy in the Junior Boot Shop, a children's shoe store in Lakeside Village. I made 50 cents an hour from which I paid my tuition. I can't say that I applied myself to school there much better than I had otherwise. Still, as with the seminary, it was a uniquely valuable experience and one from which I have profited greatly over the years, if only for the cachet in some circles for having gone to a Jesuit school. The greatest benefit, though, is the classmates I had there and whom I still see frequently, even these 55 plus years later.

By all accounts, high school is supposed to be a time of emotional and psychological confusion and so it seemed to me at the time. Having gone through what to me was a more rigorous curriculum at the seminary, I was able to skate academically for a time at SI. It wasn't until graduation, almost two years later, that they finally began to catch up to me.

There were the usual class, or clique, distinctions that seem to afflict high school life everywhere. At the top of the social pecking order were the Italian guys from North Beach whose families had businesses which provided the boys with near-new automobiles. Right under them were sons of high ranking officers in the police and fire departments, largely Irish ethnically, who tended to have slightly older automobiles. The superior athletes, in a class by themselves, were honorary members of the two upper groups. There was some overlap among groups as well.

Off by themselves were what would now be called the nerds, brainy guys who didn't get much involved in the more rambunctious aspects of adolescence. Then there was the group of the great unwashed mass of students, the non-descript middle, who had no claim to any particular notability. Within that larger group was a sub-group of marginal delinquents, guys who were not unknown to borrow a car not their own now and then. I place myself somewhere with one foot in the general group and another in the marginal delinquents.

Another way of categorizing classmates into groups was attire. The most desirable articles of clothing were McGregor unlined zipper jackets, Pendleton shirts, Price's shoes, and cashmere v-necked sweaters. Dickey suntans came later, as I recall. Status increased proportionately as the number and shades of pieces of apparel in a classmates' wardrobe increased.

Some of the Jesuits' educative efforts must have stuck on me though I can't remember anything specific. The events I remember from the period have more to do with extra-curricular activities than anything taking place in class. Once in our junior year, Municipal Railway workers went on strike. We managed to get to school OK, by hitch-hiking I suppose, but once there, a large number of us decided that we hadn't been able to make it because of the strike, and we took the day off. We all repaired to Hugh McGowan's house where we partied away the day. It was that day I realized that I had a pretty good head for alcohol because, while I imbibed my share, I was able to get through my after-school employment in the shoe store without anyone being the wiser.

A few of us from the neighborhood took the 10 Monterey bus to school each morning from 9th and Judah, accompanied by rows of seated Star of the Sea girls in their middies and pleated plaid skirts. To our hyper charged adolescent imaginations, the girls were ranked before us in row upon row of bare-to-the-waist nymphs, bereft of their middies and book bags. Further trouble was averted by our departure from the bus at 8th and Fulton where we took another up to Stanyan Street and the protective cloister of St. Ignatius. Unintentional frotteurism was reserved for the more heavily frequented, standing-room-only, 28 Alemany bus after school. That and the unbidden erections brought on by the bouncing of the vehicle—invariably announcing their presence just before one's stop—make it easier to understand why some male high school students didn't concentrate on their studies as much as their elders might have wanted them to. Raging hormones. I have wondered in later years how much the girls were aware of what was going on.

Then there were the fires. My first experience with fire was when I was four and we lived at 30th and Castro. I was up on the hill across from 570 (the site of the old quarry) with another little boy who had matches. He encouraged me to light one which I did. It set the grass afire and we took off running down Laidley Street, not bothering to stop as neighbors, who were up to what we had done, called out to us. When the fire apparatus arrived, I was standing at the front window of our house with my father watching the operation, as he commented that some kid had probably started it.

As a kid, I had a fascination with fire and matches. As a pre-teen I managed to get hold of lighter fluid and a lighter which on one occasion I set my bedroom on fire while Rose Smith was out somewhere. Ray Doherty and I had heard of the theory that lighter fluid burned so quickly it would burn off one's hands without causing any damage. I soaked my right hand in lighter fluid while Ray managed the lighter end of the operation. At the last moment I decided I didn't want to proceed but Ray felt we were too far into the experiment to quit and set the lighter aflame.

My hand caught on fire, of course, causing me to drop the bottle of lighter fluid which spilled its burning contents on the floor. We managed to smother the fire with blankets just as we heard the car approaching. We quickly turned out the lights and hopped into bed. The adults came in to check on us, and when they opened the door and turned on the light they were greeted by a smoke-filled room and two boys feigning sleep. I took full responsibility for that one because I was leaving for camp in two days which would put an end to any punishment for me, while Ray was stuck there all summer that year.

At SI, things could get tedious on rainy days. Because we couldn't eat lunch in the yards as was our usual custom, we would all have to repair to the large concrete basement of the school. To break the monotony sometimes, and create a little excitement, students would set the empty milk cartons in the metal trash cans afire. There was a lot of excitement but not really any danger of a general fire. The basement was of solid concrete construction and the cans wouldn't burn, although I don't think the arson squad would view things exactly that way. I wasn't the only one to set the fires and it wasn't my idea, but I did do it once.

Someone must have snitched me off because one of the scholastics, Mr Keith, invited me to the Jesuit residence one night to talk things over. He started talking about the fires in a friendly way, asking me if I knew anything about them, just by way of clearing things up. He assured me that there would be no negative consequences. I disavowed any knowledge of the crime. Then he took out a cigarette and asked me if I had a light. Though I had cigarettes and matches in my pocket at the time, I told the good cleric that I did not smoke. Frustrated, he told me that would be all. There is no doubt in my mind that I would have been expelled summarily had I confessed. Perhaps even then I was learning the rudiments of the job where I would spend my working life. Never again do I remember being so fascinated by fire.

Sometimes we would cut school on a fine Spring day and go to Baker's Beach. Once, as a military helicopter flew over us we gave it the single middle-finger salute. To acknowledge our salute, the pilot descended to within a few feet of our heads and revved his rotor, covering us and our clothing with sand. For some reason, never fully explained, the school decided to expel about 20 percent of our class in one stroke late in our junior year. The two criteria for expulsion seem to have been misconduct and academic inadequacy. The fact that I was not expelled at that time suggests that I was not as delinquent as I may have thought myself. Or perhaps some Jesuit saw some redeeming quality and spared me.

As I look at what I have written, it comes across as more of a confessional than a straight memoir. Writing it as I do for the later consumption of those who follow, I suppose I can offer it as lesson that even if you screw up sometimes, you are not necessarily doomed to ultimate failure. Although, for me it was a chancy business that could in many instances have tipped over the line and resulted in permanently harmful consequences. Some of my "bad boy" friends did continue in a downward spiral and did indeed come to no-good ends. My sense is that I spent my youth in a generally more forgiving time than kids today.

I'm sure there were positive productive experiences as well, even though I seem to be dwelling on the negative. I remember the Prefect of Discipline, Father Leonard, a good and fair man. For all of that, he was known to punch out errant students. The principal, Father Finnegan, was more patient with the little miscreant than he had to be. Most of the instructors were professional in their demeanor, and while I saw some of my fellow students interacting with them favorably, for myself there was always a distance, probably due to my own insecurities, masked by a wise-guy front. I never could convince myself that any of them genuinely cared about me or my welfare. When I learned as an adult of Groucho Marx's comment that he "wouldn't belong to any club that would have him as a member," I knew exactly what he meant. And I was not surprised to learn that the manic funnyman had a depressive personality.

People often refer to the teacher who turned their life around and set them on the path to a successful life career. I can't really cite such a teacher, because it was a long after my formal schooling that I started getting ambitious about much of anything. But I should mention Mr. Warren White. He taught first period English, starting at 8 am. If I missed the first bus connection I would sometimes not make it to class until 8:10 or so, a transgression which he would regularly forgive. He lived somewhere out near where I worked in Lakeside Village and he would sometimes give me a ride to work after school. On those rides, he would try to engage me intellectually about literature and plays. I wasn't really ready for what he had to say yet, but I do remember him, from among my other teachers, for having been kindly, caring and humane.

Figure 6-Senior Prom.

In the end, I didn't graduate with my class on the stage, a loss which struck my father hard. Father Richard Spohn flunked me in physics and I had to go to the Drew School that summer and make up the grade to obtain my diploma from SI. I remember the instructor at Drew's asking me what I was doing there because I had the physics down pretty well. I told her that my problem was personal.

I don't doubt that I really flunked the pertinent test which resulted in my being banned from the stage. But problems with Spohn were not unique. Other classmates I've spoken to report difficulties with him as well. And Michael Corrigan (class of 1960) captures and elaborates on Spohn's essential pomposity in his *Confessions of a Shanty Irishman.* I believe my own cocky demeanor interacting with the priest's martinet personality had much to do with the final failing grade. Guys like that never have cottoned to me. And I don't much like formal ceremonies anyway.

Most of my class was going on to college, and I wasn't, so it didn't matter much at the time. For me, the subject of college never came up—and to tell the truth I didn't bring it up. My father had gone to school to the equivalent of the fourth grade in Ireland before going to work full-time. In Rose Smith's world view, there was no sense going to college unless you were going to be a priest. The mantra growing up was —whenever we said we wanted to do something—"You can do it when you are out of high school and on your own." We looked forward to that freedom.

People have gotten higher educations under far more difficult circumstances than mine. I have come to the realization much later in life that I really don't like the classroom setting much. In a way I was too impatient with the slow pace. I've always liked to read and find out for myself. This, of course, leaves gaps in understanding which would otherwise be filled by collegial interchanges. In the end, it was my loss, though I didn't consider it so at the time.

I planned to go into the military anyway.

8 – The Army

When I graduated from high school I was 17 years old. I stood 6″1″ high and weighed 139 lbs. I spent that summer rather aimlessly, drinking milkshakes to fatten myself up, and looking forward to my 18th birthday when I would be old enough to prove my manhood by joining the army. I continued working in the shoe store but I still found time to get into some mischief. Mrs. Theriault—Herman's mother who the nuns had told us earlier not to associate with—provided us with a refuge of sorts. She worked during the day at a menial job in a French laundry which left her house unsupervised all through my later high school years and beyond. Not that we were all that bad. We did some beer drinking there and sometimes dallied with neighborhood girls.

Ray Doherty was off in the Navy and I fell under the spell of a slightly older guy named Jim who lived across the street. Jim, who was doubtless working out his own juvenile angst, was one of those people who need to manipulate others, and I suppose I was rather susceptible to his blandishments at the time

Jim and I sometimes went down to the Fillmore District where he bought marijuana—even at that early date—while I waited in the car. I didn't partake at that time. I was up to drinking beer since high school days, and holding it well, but I wasn't up for drugs. It was common practice on Friday nights in high school to acquire a six pack of beer ($1.06) and go to Golden Gate Park or some other secluded spot to imbibe. Sometimes we would get into local saloons whose proprietors tolerated younger drinkers. I can't believe, as I look back on it, that Rose Smith and my father didn't have some idea about what was going on. They came out of an Irish culture in which it was normal for young men to drink, and the saloon culture then prevalent in San Francisco would have tolerated it as well. I suspect that they more or less expected it, though they didn't say a word. That is one cultural practice which has greatly diminished, and thankfully so. I know a lot of contemporaries who didn't come out at the other end of that pipeline so successfully.

Jim and I would go to the arcades on Market Street where he encouraged me to get tattoos which today I accept as part of life, but which I still wish I didn't have. We committed a few minor misdemeanors which could have brought us to the attention of the police. I drew the line, though, when he hatched up a scheme by which I would snatch the purse of an older woman walking in Golden Gate Park and run to the top of a nearby hill where I would hand it off to him. I adamantly refused to do that one.

Dick Anthony and I would pencil the peach fuzz on our upper lips on Saturday nights and go down to the International Settlement on Pacific Street to fool around. Sometimes we got in the night clubs and sometimes the police threw us out. Already we knew about Gay San Francisco. Often I went around by myself. One night I went swimming at Sutro's by and I saw this older guy checking me out. Later I went down to Playland at the Beach and the same guy reappeared, obviously interested in more than my mind. I split. We would go to 12 Adler Place in a group where we knew we would be welcome, and we were, but we stayed in a pack to avoid any entanglements.

I once heard a Juvenile Court Judge saying that the best rehabilitation for a juvenile delinquent is not to be caught, for if apprehended he becomes inextricably involved with the justice system. That judge was right. I sometimes think of how my life would have turned out differently if a police officer had come around the corner during any number of youthful stupidities.

Jim joined the army, and the Airborne, and I followed suit. I later met him at Fort Bragg, North Carolina when he returned from Japan with the 187th Airborne Regimental Combat Team. I was at the time a respectable corporal in the 82nd Airborne and he, who was senior to me, was still a buck private, suggesting that he had had disciplinary problems along the way. I went to see him and got the distinct impression that he was not interested in visiting with me. That was the last time I ever saw him. In all honesty, I must admit that I have not always been the truest friend, myself, that I might have been.

I joined the army in November 1953. I don't know if everyone had to go through it but I remember having to talk to a psychiatrist, perhaps because of my choice of the Airborne as my preferred military specialty. Then it was off to Fort

Ord in Monterey and basic training. One thing I found out right away: city kids are not as tough as farm boys when it comes to standing up to the weather. Country people, at the time at least, were accustomed to living out-of-doors while city dwellers spent much of their time protected from the elements. And in the army, during your waking hours, you were almost always out-of-doors. My hands were so cold one morning on the firing range that I was unable to peel an orange. I remember thinking at the time that people came to Monterey for vacations and here I was, nearly freezing to death. It seemed to me that the army always picked the most uncomfortable spots for their bases, hot or cold.

It was in the army that for the first time in my life I had anything to do with people were not Catholic and not mostly of Irish background. Everyone, from all over the country ended up in basic training at Fort Ord. In all the activity and stress, I didn't even notice, and made friends on the basis of natural affinity rather than neighborhood associations. Another thing I came to realize is that not everyone from California had an urban background. Indeed, I'd say that the majority of the California recruits would prefer country music to pop. (Any place I was ever in the army, the guy who owned the radio would invariably tune it to country.)

There were three guys from Farmersville, down by Visalia, who showed up the first day, unfamiliar with what I thought were the basic conventions of civilization. Lean, strong and wiry guys, quiet and fiercely loyal to each other, they reminded me of the southerners I met later at Ft. Benning and Bragg. There were also Latino guys, all of whom seemed to claim they hailed from "L.A., man." Some of them had volunteered for the Airborne also, so we got along well and went on to Fort Benning together.

Another thing about basic training was the sickness. It is a fact of military history that more soldiers have died of disease than ever were ever killed in battle. When recruits are drawn from all over and put together where they can exchange their various germs, it makes for a sickly environment. A recruit named Moss, a few bunks away from me, a draftee with a recent graduate degree in industrial psychology, 26 years old, came down with meningitis and did not survive.

The training company was made up of RAs (regular army), young enlistees like me, and draftees who ran older and often had college time. For some reason, while I was still attracted to the "bad boys" I often found myself in the company of these older, more educated draftees. When I got to the regular army Airborne, there were fewer of this group, but what few there were I managed to find.

Training consisted of all the running, marching and weapons familiarization, long, sleepless hours, and harassment by low IQ cadre that formed one's induction into the military at the time. During the first eight weeks training I contracted an infection which settled in my "weak Irish chest." For the remainder of the first eight weeks, I was coughing and hacking, and spitting up bloody phlegm.

Newfound friends shied away from me for fear of contagion. I was alone and sick and instead of building me up, the rigorous physical exertions broke me down. It was all I could do to complete the first eight weeks of basic training.

We were given a short leave between basic and advanced infantry training which I spent at Rose Smith's house. I spent the days of my leave—it was one of those warm winter periods that come to San Francisco in February—sunning myself on the grass at Big Rec in Golden Gate Park. That and the home cooking seem to have turned the trick. For when I returned for the second eight weeks I was able to do anything physically that anyone else could do and more than most. (The fire which does not destroy us only makes us strong.) It was the first time since my session with malnutrition at St. Catherine's at Benicia that I felt that I fully approached what I would call a normal level of health and strength. After that, there was no looking back.

Sometime in April or May, 1954, I emplaned in Monterey—my first plane ride—to Fort Benning, Georgia, and jump school.

9 – Jump School

In 1954 I had never heard of the term "culture shock," even as I got a good dose of it. In a few hours, by my reckoning, I was whisked by military transport from the only world I had known, the relatively sophisticated environs of the Bay Area to the completely alien world of Fort Benning in South Georgia. The climate was different, the foliage was different, the soil was different and the people were certainly different. I arrived steeled to handle anything they might hand me—to the jeers of jump school candidates who had arrived a few weeks earlier. If they had survived well enough to harass newcomers, I reasoned, I could make it myself.

My first real problem with the cultural divide occurred almost immediately when I was assigned to KP (kitchen police). I had seen enough of mess hall personnel during basic training to figure out that cooks in training companies were not the brightest stars in the military firmament, though some of them—for the first time in their life with someone down the social scale from them—might have considered themselves so.

In any event, I was on my best behavior, intending to do my best not to rile any of my supervisors. Right off the bat, I had a cook screaming at me. The message, as best I could make out from his tantrum, was that I was as stupid as anyone he had ever seen. It was the Georgia accent. He had told me to go out and get something he pronounced as a "jiabrush." One word. I didn't have the foggiest notion of what the man was talking about. In the end, I found out that he was referring to a "G.I. Brush," a common enough scrubbing instrument, known to everyone, even me. I suppose I must have gotten the hang of the accent because I didn't have any more trouble in that line. (When I returned home from the service three years later, my sister Nancy commented, "Kevin, you sound just like an Okie." In the broadest sense the term, "Okie" in the San Francisco lexicon of the time, was applied to any Californian not from one of the close-in Bay Area counties excluding Alameda.)

Jump school was hard physically. For one thing you had to run whenever you were outside a barracks building and, in a world where most business is conducted out-of doors, that is a lot of running. Beyond that, there were the regular PT sessions to build up strength, agility and endurance. The thinking was that the better shape you were in, the less likely you were to injure yourself in a bad landing. It's true. At one point, I think, some kind of primal monkey gene kicked in and I found myself clambering around in all sorts of high places without worrying about falling. Not everyone made it. I remember one guy, a real tough cowboy from Montana, who simply couldn't do the required number of pull-ups. As the numbers winnowed down, group cohesiveness emerged, making the last part of the training enjoyable if still rigorous.

Figure 7-Before the Jump.

It took something to jump out the door of that C-119 the first time—or indeed any time—from a thousand feet up or so. I buoyed myself up with the belief that the army really didn't want to get me killed after all the money they put into my training. As a statistical proposition that was probably true. I'm sure, though, that the army had factored in a certain amount of inventory shrinkage and didn't have any particular interest in keeping me alive as an individual.

Figure 8-After the Jump.

In any event, we made our five jumps and one sunny Saturday we were awarded our coveted "wings." The next day we were off duty, and I remember a bunch of us parading around the main post, our wing emblazoned chests stuck out manfully. I don't know if we were actually looking for a fight but we had convinced ourselves that we would have acquitted ourselves well against any number of "straightlegs," non-airborne soldiers. It was a ridiculous proposition, as any number of marines, whipped by skinny sailors, could attest. We ended up going to a movie—"The Boy on a Dolphin" as I recall—quite a letdown after all. I don't know what kind of transformation I had been expecting but the next day it was the same old me.

Then it was on to Ft. Bragg, North Carolina, where I was assigned to a rifle company, Company E, 504 AIR, 82nd Airborne Division. Thereafter we had to make a jump every couple of months or more to maintain our jump pay of $50 extra a month. I jumped more than that, particularly when I got to Germany, and ended up with 38 jumps.

If the seminary had given me a glimpse of the prototypical boarding prep school, Company E gave me a version of the "From Here To Eternity" peacetime army experience of the period. Much of the army at that time was comprised of draftees, usually older, often more educated, and temporary soldiers, who knew they were going to move on to other pursuits. These citizen-soldiers were not so easily pushed around. They had their own ideas about things and were less receptive to the chicken-shit features of the regular army. To my way of thinking, they had a moderating influence on the regular army traditions. But in the airborne, as volunteers, we were almost all regular army and the old ways still prevailed.

We lived in wooden two-story pre-World War 2 barracks at the time, one platoon to a barracks. Our main professional activity was training. That usually consisted of a daily march far out on the aptly named Longstreet Road in the humid heat of the North Carolina summer. We were so full of salt pills that the creases in our jump boots turned white from sweat. Presumably, we did some training at the hike's end but I don't remember learning anything much. I never could get the bubbles on the 60 millimeter mortar or 30 caliber machine gun to level properly. But then there wasn't much competition in that regard from most of my fellow soldiers, so there was little incentive to learn. (I thought about these things later when I watched the young troopers on television in the opening days of the Iraq War, manipulating complicated computer-operated weaponry. They were so obviously much better trained and motivated than we had been.)

The most trying part of the daily exercise was the dry march back on the long, hot road. There were no water faucets in the boondocks, so we had only the water we could carry, and that was often expended in the early part of the day. We finally figured out that we could carry extra canteens. The weight was unwelcome in the early stages of the march but it paid off on the way back.

Soldiers in that outfit spent a great deal of effort figuring out ways to avoid the marches. A visit to sick call would do it, or some kind of detail which kept you past the time of departure. If you simply avoided the departure, you had to figure out what to do during the day. You would stand out in the sparsely populated company area and soon come under official scrutiny requiring you to account for your presence. One soldier figured out a solution to that problem. He acquired a clip-board somewhere and if anyone questioned him as he went about, he told them he had been detailed to check the level in the coal bins which adjoined each of the company barracks.

There were all the usual activities one would associate with regular army barracks life. The largest identifiable group, when I think about it, was white southerners of Scots-Irish extraction. I wasn't aware of it at the time that this group made up the backbone of the then—and now?—military. They tended to be quiet types and made up the larger part of the group considered "field" soldiers, as distinguished from "garrison" soldiers who kept their uniforms sharp and were disinclined to get dirty in the boondocks.

For me, the army was a lark or an adventure. I had never had any intention to re-up. I didn't know what I wanted to do with my life; I just more or less assumed that I would wake up someday at 40 years old, the CEO of one of the big corporations or something. For these southern white guys the army was a step up from whatever they had going before. I remember them disdaining a return to civilian life and some dead-end factory job. They were tough guys.

There were also a lot of African-Americans in the outfit. They tended to have enlisted from areas near Ft. Bragg, attracted, I suppose, by the sharp uniforms and, like the southern whites, by the chance of better jobs than they could hope to have in civilian life. I don't remember them as being so inclined to favor life in the field. Perhaps 20 percent of our barracks were black guys. Maybe 50 percent southern white and then the rest made up of "the rest of us."

Everybody seemed to get along in the barracks. The southern whites and the blacks, even those from Philly, had their etiquette worked out. They moved around each other in polite circles. I recall that the blacks tended to keep a respectful, almost fearful, distance from certain whites. There were two little guys from Tennessee of whom they were terrified. (Probably with good reason. One of the guys named at the time as one of the killers of Emmett Till had recently been discharged from Fox Company next door. At least that was the story at the time.)

Being from San Francisco, with no real history of the type of overt racial separation then prevalent in the South, I, like the farm boys from Michigan, and the cowboys from Montana, seemed to get along with everybody. At Fort Bragg we, just didn't give much of a thought to race, though I'm sure there must have been undercurrents of which I was unaware. On the surface we got along fine. On occasion, troopers fell out on the company street to resolve conflicts with a little "knuckle drill" but I don't remember any fights with an inter-racial cast. For all of the racial amity, when payday came and it was time to go to town, the races separated. I don't remember ever seeing any black soldiers on Hay Street in Fayetteville.

I suppose payday best exemplified the old-army aspect of our unit. Everyone had been broke for weeks and, with cash in hand, the dam broke. We were paid off in cash in the day room, then, as if on cue, the officers disappeared. One of the barracks turned into a gambling casino, run by a black master sergeant who was assigned to the company but who I never saw in the company except on payday. For the rest of us it was off to Fayetteville and the beer joints on Hay Street. Images of "From Here to Eternity" immediately come to mind. There was a lot of beer drinking and later there were the whores at the Prince Charles Hotel for those so inclined. And many of the troops were so inclined.

Payday over, the troops returned sheepishly to their barracks, broke, but with "three hots and a cot" to sustain them to the next payday when they would repeat the process again. For three weeks of each month, a large part of the company would be broke. This gave rise to the court-martial-worthy practice of loan sharking. It was easy to loan out money at five dollars "for seven and a half back payday." Later in the month the rate would increase to "ten dollars back." A hoarded bottle of whiskey would go for as much as $20 a week before payday. (They are called "payday loans" in civil society these days, and they can be obtained anyplace there are large aggregations of low-income people.)

Given the natural frailty of man, it was an easy line to get into. I held back my pay one month and loaned it out in later weeks at the going rate. In the following months, my poke multiplied so that I had enough to spend on myself and still had plenty to put out at interest. I soon came to the conclusion, though, that that just wasn't me. The loan shark can't really have any friends, I came to discover, so I closed up shop and rejoined the hoi polloi.

Friends could be untrue. There was this one guy, Sam, from New York, from one barracks over, with whom I had gone through Jump School at Benning. One day toward the end of the month we wanted to go up to go to main post and go swimming and grab a meal. Sam didn't have any money, he said, so I sponsored him with my last remaining cash. Another way to make do at the end of the month was to run errands for others for a tip. That night I wanted something from the enlisted men's club so I offered to fetch something for another barrack-mate if he would stake me to whatever it was. When I arrived at the club, there was Sam in regal splendor, alone in a booth, with a large spread of food and beer before him.

I have had many good friends in my life and I treasure them, but I also recognize that I have sometimes been a better friend to some people than they were to me, particularly in the early years. On reflection, I'd rather be in my boots than theirs. (Sam later took a short discharge and reenlisted for six years to go to Japan and to make a re-enlistment bonus of a few hundred dollars. He was a New York street guy and didn't have the makings of a soldier so I can't see him as having any future luck in the army.) I must admit that I have taken some pleasure over the years when some of the slicker guys, who may have put things over on me when I was younger, have fallen behind in the sweepstakes of life.

The residents of Fayetteville really didn't want much to do with the soldiers and you can understand why, particularly those with daughters. The girls themselves were very wary of soldiers. You had the feeling in town that there was this whole other world that you were not a part of. It was a rare soldier who could crack that shell and make his way into the heart of a daughter of that town. These Lotharios we held in high esteem.

I remember one guy from some northeast city, probably New York, who located, courted, and married the battalion commander's daughter to better his condition until he could shed himself of the army, and the daughter. He was a real operator. Once he attached himself at the end of the pay line for several months on end—until he was found out—and collected a dollar from each soldier to pay for a new pool table for the day room, which of course never appeared. (The two groups of soldiers who always knew what was going on were the blacks and those from New York City. They had some kind of internal group informational networks.)

I did get a chance to see a part of the South aside from beer joints, honky-tonks, and gas station white liquor stops. My friend from Michigan, Darwin Wayne Henry, had a car and we would sometimes range through the back-country. (Again, it was like the seminary and the regular army. I was given an opportunity to get a glimpse of the South unadorned, an experience which has enriched my understanding of much I have read about the region since that time.)

One day in late 1954, Darwin and I had the day off in mid-week for some reason. We were in our civilian clothes and ready to head for town when the orders came down that a hurricane was expected and everyone was to gather in the single-story mess hall. Considering ourselves not covered by the order, Darwin and I climbed out the back window of the mess hall and made our way to town in the middle of what proved to be a major hurricane. (I have since seen films of that storm in hurricane retrospectives.) Indestructible as we were, we drove through a landscape of falling trees to Fayetteville where businesses had closed down. We didn't really have so much conventional fun that day. I remember being in the back country someplace. The electricity was out and we finally found an old hand-pump gas station where we could fuel the car.

After about a year of regular barracks life, an officer at the morning formation asked for volunteers who were over six feet in height. Now the rule in the army is to never volunteer. But I had had enough of eating the dust on Longstreet Road and mortar bubbles that wouldn't line up, so I took a flyer and stepped forward.

That's how I ended up in the honor guard/drill team platoon of "America's Guard of Honor."

10 – Honor Guard

When I observe the athletic prowess of young people these days, I wonder if they might be some different superior breed of animal. We all had roller skates when I was a kid, and I got pretty good with them, but the things young guys do with skateboards far exceed anything in our repertoire. And windsurfing. There were surfers then, of course, but when you add a sail, the forces of physics multiply. Add the element of doing it in ocean rollers, and it defies my ability to comprehend.

When I occasionally see military drill teams on television as part of some promotional or patriotic film, however, I say "We could do that." When you drill together with an M-1 rifle morning and afternoon day-after-day for months on end, you get pretty good. The rifle becomes as light as a broomstick in your hands and the muscle memory eventually kicks in. It's all about the cadence of the beat. Once you get it going it's easy to keep together, or at least it becomes so.

Figure 9-Honor Guard

That's what we did—that and keep our uniforms and equipment shaped up—and not much else. We had a barracks of our own which we kept shipshape, and each day we would assemble on the regimental parade field and drill ourselves to exhaustion. There was a lieutenant in charge of the platoon but the real supervision was done by a Sergeant First Class Hernandez. He didn't drill himself as I recall, but was more or less our father figure. We all got pretty good but the stars were a couple of black guys, one Sergeant Johnson in particular.

(It was my introduction to the" dozens" and Staggerlee. Some of us would take turns counting the cadence in that format and I got pretty good at it. I still remember parts of them, specifically the "signifying monkey" who harassed the lion from the safety of his perch in the tree and when the monkey fell out of the tree, the lion "jumped on him with all four feet.")

We were quintessential garrison soldiers. There would be no more Longstreet Road, though we did have to participate in occasional overnight and week-long field maneuvers. I must say, for the sloppy guy I am—as my wife Jeannie would be the first to attest—I took to the regimented life very well. I was promoted to corporal around this time. Each week, the winner of the area and personal inspection would earn a three-day pass. For a while, I won the pass regularly. The very obsessive behavior which drove me to the perfection which won the pass, also drove me to spend it, not in town or off somewhere, but in the barracks, getting ready for the next week. The spell was broken when we went to Detroit to drill in some parade or other and I met a girl. On our return, I remained shaped up though not to the obsessive degree as before.

Out-of-the-area trips were some of the side benefits to the job. One time we went to Wilmington, North Caarolina to drill in the annual Azalea Festival. It was a big deal in the town that week and we wowed them with our drill as was customary. The town leaders more or less had to invite us to their ball. (I suppose that only applied to the white guys because I never remember socializing with the black guys off duty.) It was one of those Southern cotillion type balls where all the southern belles showed up in their long formal gowns and corsages. We soon got the message, though, about where we stood in the social pecking order. The girls, with their caps set for officers, wouldn't give us the time of day. So we departed the ball and went honky-tonking in the joints down town.

Another time, we went to New York where we drilled on television's "The Soldiers Parade" with Polly Bergen as hostess, my first glimpse at the inherent phoniness of the show business world. There was a great deal of elaborate hugging among people who hadn't seen each other for at least a few hours. It was the same sort of over-the-top displays of affection at socially incestuous Nob Hill gatherings.

Figure 10-New York, New York.

In our off-time we prowled Broadway, ending up acting like fools in what I now know to have been Hell's Kitchen. Maybe there are guardian angels after all. I picked up a girl in the Metropole Bar who tried to set me up to be rolled by her thuggish hotel employee accomplice, a variation of the badger game. I didn't know that expression yet but I figured out the game and avoided that trap. Sergeant Hernandez, our leader and father figure, shocked my moral sensibilities when he returned from his adventures on the town and reported without any shame that he had submitted to a sex act with a man, for $10, to restore his depleted purse. What a town!

It was about that time that we got a new lieutenant, a West Pointer named Lt. Hicks, and I received a lesson in the gulf between an educated book officer and the world of the enlisted man. One day, the lieutenant informed Sgt. Johnson, our best rifle-handler, that he would report to the parade ground at such-and-such time to acquaint some friends of the lieutenant from West Point with the finer points of our drill. Sergeant Hernandez intervened and told Sergeant Johnson not to report as ordered, informing the lieutenant that our drill moves were our own and in effect copyrighted. We did not share them with anyone. The lieutenant said to Hernandez: "I told Sergeant Johnson to be on the parade ground in the morning, Sergeant Hernandez." In front of all of us, Hernandez replied "I told him not to, lieutenant, and I can kick his ass, and you can't." They are not wimpy men who keep America safe.

On another occasion, we were on maneuvers out in the boondocks and our platoon was assigned road security details. A black guy, another Johnson, and I were posted at the intersection of two roads with orders to stop and investigate any vehicle that tried to pass. It was night—dark as it can get only in the country on a moonless night. We were tasked to each take two hour shifts on the road block while the other rested in a nearby pup tent. In the middle of the night I had finished one of my shifts and I returned to the tent to inform Johnson that it was his turn. He chose to remain in the tent which was fine with me.

Sometime later a jeep hurried up to the road block and stopped. A shouted voice demanded to know who was supposed to be on the post. "Me, lieutenant," Johnson shouted back from the tent, "I knew it was you." "How could you know it's me?" demanded the lieutenant, "It's pitch black out here." Johnson responded: "Because you are the only one crazy enough to be out at this time of night, lieutenant." I hope the lieutenant made field grade by the time that the Vietnam War hotted up or that he changed his leadership style. Otherwise, he would have been fragged for sure.

The whole officer thing eluded me at the time. It might be because I felt I couldn't measure up, but I think not. It was a culture, at least in the regular army at the time, which remains distasteful to me to this day. One time I was detailed "to guard" a large silver regimental bowl or cup at the officer's club during some kind of formal reception. I watched from parade rest as arriving officers greeted each other. There is no other way to say it: the officers—and their wives—smilingly groveled their way up the ranks, while accepting the obeisance of those below. It was all jolly and fun-filled, and a bit sick, even to my untutored sensibility.

(I saw the same sort of thing later in Germany. Our division commander, a major general who we hardly ever even saw, was a god in our little firmament. I found out later that he had served in combat with distinction during World War Two. Our division had gotten the entire army forces in Germany restricted to post for reasons which will be discussed later. Anyway, the commanding general of all European forces, a three-star general, came to our *kaserne* to lay down the law. As the entire command stood in formation, our two-star general hopped around like a lackey, opening doors and saluting the three-star general like a fool. I later thought of re-enlisting for OCS but that scene weighed heavily on the negative side of the scale.)

It was time to move on. The word came down that volunteers were being sought for the 11th Airborne Division at Fort Campbell Kentucky which was being rotated to Germany on something called Operation Gyroscope. One of the necessary conditions, though, was that the soldier involved had to have 18 months, or something like that, left on his enlistment. I wanted to go but I had only about a year left to go. So I paid a friend in the orderly room—an entrepreneurial guy from Montana who I'm sure went on to a successful career in business--$10 to get placed on the transfer order.

Then it was off to Fort Campbell and eventually on to Germany. From then on at every replacement depot I went through, on up to my re-embarkation from Germany back to the States, somebody would ask me "How did you get here with so little time to do?" I said "I don't know. They just sent me."

11 – Fort Campbell

During that time, the army was introducing specialist ranks, in an effort, I suppose, to reward technical proficiency. The regular supervisory ranks of corporal and the various grades of sergeant were retained, but most people, including me, were converted to specialist ratings corresponding to the pay grades of the supervisory ranks we had held. The regular supervisory ranks were considered preferable, though, because they had a command element. I'd bet the same distinction still obtains.

For some reason unknown to me—perhaps it was my buddy in the orderly room at Bragg—my orders listed me as a corporal, and that is how I arrived at Fort Campbell. Somebody at the Repo Depo (Replacement Depot) asked if there were any corporals in the shapeless crowd of replacements before him. Recognizing that this had to be a better deal than that which was in store for the others, I stepped out. That's how I got the assignment as the permanent CQ (charge of quarters) at the Repo Depo headquarters.

The job entailed managing the company office from 5 pm each night until about 8 or 9 am the next day when the Company Commander and the regular office crew arrived. I had a jeep assigned to me and in effect was the commanding officer of the company during the night. Because of the long hours the detail entailed, the schedule called for one night on and then two days and nights off, which left plenty of free time to get into mischief. I didn't have to stand any formations and was free to come and go as I pleased.

As at other times in my life, I seemed to have my foot in two worlds, one respectable and the other less so. I developed some friends who you might call intellectuals. They were interested, and I joined them—perhaps prefiguring a prominent later interest of mine—in the history of the Old West. If real life were a war movie I would have been the guy they called "Doc."

On the other hand, I liked to hang out with the guys who partied. One time a few of us decided to go to Evansville Indiana, a reportedly open town. To get there, we had to drive though Kentucky. Kentucky was a dry state at the time, but you could buy liquor at state-run stores in Tennessee which were to be found along the border. That's what we did. We bought a bottle in Tennessee and made our way into Kentucky. We hadn't gone far when we were pulled over on a country road by a constable driving an Oldsmobile.

He took us to the house of a local justice of the peace who "tried" us for transporting liquor on the highway. I remember that the justice was an old man with holes cut in his slippers from which his toes protruded. There was not enough to pay all our bail so I spent the night in Madisonville, Kentucky jail until my friends could return with bail. My mouth might have had something to do with it also because it was clear to me that we had been "duckponded," as traffic officers say, when we were seen leaving the liquor store and crossing the state line. I never did get to Evansville, Indiana.

By this time I had accumulated enough leave time that I could come home for a visit. I hitch-hiked from North Carolina to San Francisco to give my sister Maureen away at her wedding. My father wouldn't do it, largely because she was marrying an Italian. There was a certain rigid distrust among some of that generation of Irish toward other ethnic groups, particularly those who could get a sun tan. The phenomenon was not so pronounced in San Francisco as in large eastern cities where there was a lot more inter-ethnic competition for jobs. Growing up in San Francisco it was the custom on St. Patrick's Day to pinch members of one's circle who were not wearing green. I later befriended a slightly older Jewish guy from New York who said that in his youth, if you didn't wear green on St. Paddy's Day (as they called it back East), you would get punched in the head at the very least, and it didn't matter who your were. (Russell Baker records the identical experience in Baltimore in his memoir *Growing Up*.) In the end my father and Vince became great friends, all of which goes to show that propinquity can give birth to tolerance if behaviors are compatible.

I sometimes say I hitch-hiked across the entire country for dramatic affect but I actually made the trip by a combination of hitch-hiking and "hops" on military planes which were free for service personnel on a first-come-first-served basis when available. I remember one long swatch of hitch-hiking through Texas when there were apparently no hops available. One of my rides was from three guys in an old car, who, as I think about it, may have been on the lam. They certainly weren't looking for work. On the road, I hid my cash in the back of a camera I had then. Not too smart when you think about it. I hadn't yet heard of the trooper who hid his money in his jump boot, and when a prostitute enquired as to why he left one boot on before they got down to business, he told her that he had a wooden foot.

We picked up an older Mexican guy with a suitcase outside Eagle Pass Texas within sight of the border. His entire extended family was waiting with him by the side of the road as he hitched. It was pretty clear that he was a recent arrival in the country. When we stopped to pick him up, the family had an impromptu send off-party with kisses and hugs, reminiscent of bon voyage parties I had seen, before he entered the vehicle. He didn't speak a word of English except to communicate that he was headed for San Jose, California. I like to think that he is now the paterfamilias of a large respectable South Bay family.

Back at Fort Campbell, it was really a humdrum existence militarily, as the Division made preparations to move overseas. I had a friend in the company, whose home was nearby in Tennessee. He had a brand new 1955 Buick Century on which he was making payments. He got in some type of a scrape involving a gun in a honky-tonk near his home and with the fine imposed and all he would have been unable to keep up the payments. So I took the car off his hands and assumed the payments. There I was, a nineteen year old kid with a new V-eight Buick Century and little to hold me back. I would make frequent forays to Nashville about 50 miles away, tearing at over 100 miles an hour along what would now be considered secondary roads. Young people should not be allowed out of the house.

One night I was on my own and went to a skating rink in Nashville where I met a girl. I had known girls before, of course, but I had always been uncomfortable in their presence and had never had what you would call a real "girl friend." During the seminary days it was out of the question (though some managed it) and at Rose Smith's people didn't date until they started taking out the girl they married. The whole Catholic thing was mixed up in it as well.

I was totally unequipped to deal with a real relationship with a girl. Anyway, I now had a girl friend. I was probably considered a good catch at first by a 17-year-old kid of that time and place, with my new Buick and fancy Airborne uniform. It was doomed not to last, though, and it didn't. She came to the realization first and moved away—with a guy I knew, a career soldier from the San Joaquin Valley who I used to drive to town in my car. She married him. She later divorced the guy and married the MP who came in response to her call about a domestic dispute in their Nashville home. Still later she divorced the MP as well. At the time I was devastated, as only a prideful, insecure, immature adolescent can be. I eventually came to see it for the childish infatuation that it was, but for a time my pride was terribly hurt.

With my free-ranging army assignment at the time, I didn't pay much attention to the need for passes to leave the post. Fort Campbell was an open post so you could leave by one of the back roads and nobody would be the wiser as long as you didn't call attention to yourself by some misbehavior away from the post. I was in town every night, trying to salvage what was a hopeless situation at best. Late one night, I was returning to post and I suppose I was speeding because an officer tried to stop me. I wasn't even aware that he was after me. He took down my red, enlisted men's post license number and turned me in.

The result was that I had to stand for a summary court martial. I beat the charge because it was my word against his and— as I think about it—it was a pretty chicken-shit thing for him to become involved in. So I was transferred to work at the Publications Warehouse from where all forms, and special and general orders were issued to the divisional units. There I worked along with two PFCs under the supervision of the civilians who ran the operation. That still didn't stop me from sneaking out at night.

As the day of the division's departure neared, I turned the Buick back to its original owner, a little more worn and torn than when I received it. It was a low time for me. I was bumped out of my reverie for a time by the circumstances surrounding our departure. Some dim bulb thought it would be a good idea to send the officers ahead by train to the

New York port of embarkation. Most of the senior NCOs, who tended to be married and had families, were probably seeing to their own families' departure.

In any case, the whole of Fort Campbell Kentucky was left to the tender mercies of the lower ranks. I had never seen anything like it before. (I had not yet read Golding's *Lord of the Flies.*) With the discipline relaxed, the thin veneer of civilization was ripped off. Everyone went nuts. There was a palpable feeling of lawlessness in the air. I remember they wrecked the enlisted men's club among other depredations. People were running around shouting for no good reason I could discern, other than they were able to. (I was on CQ duty that night in the company orderly room and didn't become involved except as an amazed spectator.)

I saw the same type of phenomenon 20 years later during the San Francisco Police Strike. With the command structure effectively bypassed or neutralized during the job action, the crazies—the lowest common denominator—emerged as informal leaders as the more sensible officers hung back or took subordinate roles. Disorder ensued.

There were no repercussions to the riot—for that's what it was—at Ft. Campbell, and the next day we were all on trains and headed for New York and the troop ship.

Next stop, Augsburg, Germany.

12 - Germany

We arrived at Augsburg, Germany in the Spring of 1955, and I was assigned in charge of Publications at Division Headquarters in *Flak Kaserne*. The first thing to be noticed was that the facilities, built in Hitler's Germany in the 1930s, were far superior to anything I had seen in the U.S Army. Anyplace I had been in the army, rifle racks were locked to make sure the weapons didn't disappear. The built-in racks in Flak had been designed with no way to lock the rifles in. I suppose there is not much profit in stealing weapons in a totalitarian society.

In the States I had worked for civilians in Publications as more or less a warehouseman. The civilians didn't go overseas with us, of course, so I found myself as a corporal, in charge of the operation there. Working with me were two privates, Gary Falkner, from Dodge City, Kansas, and Irby McInnis from Gulfport, Mississippi. Later I was promoted to staff sergeant in keeping with my new position.

We soon realized that when our predecessors departed, they left behind cabinets full of ration cards, both for liquor and cigarettes. The possibilities occurred to us immediately. In the states, if you wanted liquor or cigarettes you just went and bought them. In Europe, where there was a potential for a black market involving the German people, liquor and cigarette rations to the military had to be rationed by a system of accountable numbered forms. When we entered our headquarters, there were the accountable forms, just sitting there in file cabinets. We didn't have to sign for them when we took over to accept responsibility for them; we just had the potentially valuable forms. I wish I could say that I made a million dollars which I quietly shipped home but I can't.

While the temptation was there, and with it the potential to make a lot of money, we didn't really take advantage of it. We chiseled a bit around the edges by giving cards to friends. (A ration card for cigarettes could go for $20 on the black market.) But we didn't make it a business. The prospect of the military prison at Fort Leavenworth loomed too large in our imaginations. Even today, as this is being written (April 2009) there are stories in the press about officers returning from Iraq with millions of stolen dollars being tried for the thefts. A generation ago it was the Army Sergeant-major and other master-sergeants running R&R operations in Vietnam who were prosecuted for major financial defalcations on their watch. (One of those named had been a platoon sergeant of mine at Fort Bragg and I could believe everything said about him.)

The German workers at the *kaserne* had an insatiable appetite for anything American, even scrap lumber and wooden vegetable crates which they spirited away to make their morning fires at the risk of arrest if they were caught. The war had ended not all that long before and there was still hardship aplenty, and some hard feelings were very close to the surface.

Our division, comprised as it was of regular soldier volunteers, had a very low mean average age, with all that implies. Once in Germany, and away from home, many of the young troopers went nuts. Soldiers would go to town and get drunk. They would jump from roofs and generally act up at the expense of the German people. There were a lot of arrests for rape, as I recall. In the end, their behavior caused an international incident which resulted in all military forces in Germany to be restricted to quarters until things could be sorted out.

I said "they" because I did not become involved in these shenanigans because I was nursing a broken heart and, by that time, pretty much just wanted to go home and get out of the army. I later met a German immigrant to the United States who had a little coffee shop on my beat in the Richmond District. He told me he had been working in a factory near Augsburg at the time and that he and his fellow workers considered forming vigilante groups to protect themselves from the soldiers.

I did get out a bit, though. Gary Falkner was married to his Louella and they had married quarters off the *kaserne.* The army did not provide housing for other than NCOs so Gary rented quarters on his own situated in a rural setting far from the center of military activity. It was attached to a *gasthouse* in the countryside where as I recall the people didn't speak any English. I would socialize with him out there and I got look at German life as it was. The people were more accepting of us as Americans than those in town.

Sometimes we would go together to the big *biergardens* in town where, then as now, large numbers of German families would assemble in massive halls to drink beer and sing rousing songs. *"In Munchen steed ein haufbrau haus, ein, schvie,sofa!* (rendered phonetically.) The *biergartens* were also good places to meet girls of other than the bargirl type. One young blonde I met there, gorgeous she was, promised to be more than compliant but I backed off. Even her mother approved of the deal and that was the problem. I was stayed from further pursuit when I learned that they both wanted a boat ride to the United States, and what better way than as the dependent of a U.S. military man. I can't blame them for that, for I imagine life was still pretty hard. But it was not for me.

All in all, life was pretty good. As a sergeant, I lived in the bachelor NCO quarters and didn't have to make any formations. The quarters were better than anything I had seen in the U.S., even better than officers' quarters I had seen before. We all had luxuriously furnished private rooms upstairs and a common restaurant/bar on the ground floor. For a time I flirted with the idea of reenlisting for Officers Candidate School, and if I could have been convinced that life could go on as it was, I might have done so. I knew, though, that things could change fast in the army, through one's own misbehavior or pure bad luck. The prospect of finishing a long enlistment as a private soldier in a rifle company, or worse, did not appeal to me at all.

Not all of the trouble was caused by the troops. I know there were cautions about damaging trees on maneuvers because severe compensations would have to be paid to the Germans. And there were stories about German prostitutes who cried rape, when soldiers shorted them on their fees. I heard of guys, and more than one, who received sentences of 20 years in Leavenworth in this way.

Figure 11-Coming Home.

As it was, I don't think I spent more than eight months in Germany before heading home. On the troopship returning to the States, I ran into some guys I hadn't seen since basic training. After basic, we spread to the winds and those of us who had ended up in Germany, no matter what the unit, were due for discharge on about the same date, thus we were headed home together. Some of them were people I hadn't seen for three years. As a staff sergeant I was the biggest frog in that small enlisted pond. Staff Sergeant was about as high as one could expect to go in the army in one hitch at that time. I noticed that some of the guys who had been stars in basic training were returning home as buck privates. From the shadow of PFC stripes remaining on their fatigue sleeves—obviously removed after they had been busted, one could read the story of turbulent, unsuccessful army careers.

The race is not always to the swift.

13 – The Lost Years

One Sunday in Germany, an enterprising New York auto dealer showed up at *Flak Kaserne* and put on a promotional car show. The idea was for soldiers to order cars and start paying for them from Germany, presumably at a reduced cost, to be picked up in New York on their return. The vehicle used in the display was a red and white 1955 Chevrolet convertible, the first V-eight Chevie made. I decided on the spot that I had to have one.

I was pretty flush. I had my sergeant's pay to which was added overseas and jump pay, and I had few expenses at the time. If I took my discharge in New York—instead of returning to my place of enlistment in California—I would receive $600 in travel pay. With what I had saved and would save, I could almost pay off the car the day I bought it. That's what I did. (It was not a good financial decision. I was as yet unacquainted with the concept "all hat and no cattle.")

I was discharged in Fort Dix, New Jersey in November 1956, went immediately to New York City where I picked up the car, and headed out across the country. (The model was 1956 by then—they had no V-8s in stock at the time, so I settled for a six—a fact which may have saved my life considering how I was prone to drive those days.)

Winter was setting in and I headed south. Had I been quicker on the uptake, I might have taken advantage of an opportunity that could have put me in jail. I stopped for a time in a cheap hotel in Nashville, the rooms of which were separated by dividers which didn't run all the way to the ceiling. There was a coffee shop attached to the hotel, run by a woman, where you could get a drink of liquor in a coffee cup in the otherwise dry town. The woman's husband held court there daily. It seems he was a former Chief of Police of Nashville though you wouldn't know it by his overalls and general country mien. He engaged me in conversation once and mentioned that a young fellow with a car with New York license plates could make a fine piece of change driving a load of liquor down to Memphis.

Figure 12-Chevy and Friend.

I toyed with the idea but rejected it. And just as well, for I was far down the road on my way out of town before I realized it may have been a set-up. Had I taken him up on his offer, I wonder if it would have gotten me into a career in the illegal adult beverage industry in the South. I think not. It strikes me that moonshining is pretty much a home industry and that there isn't much room for an incidental passer-through. It's just as likely that he was related to some of the folks who set us up on our way to Evansville, Indiana a year so before, and I might just as soon have ended up on a southern road gang without a car.

I proceeded west along the old Route 66, headed home. I had a laugh-out-load moment all by myself while passing through Arizona or New Mexico. It was flat desert all around except for a large butte in the far distance. As I got closer, I could see that somebody had climbed up there and written in large white letters: "Jesus Saves." As I got closer still, I could see that someone else had climbed up later and in smaller letters underneath had written "string."

Home from the wars, I moved in with my sister, Maureen and her family, and for want of anything else to do I returned to the shoe store even though I knew it was not for me. My peers there were all young married men with families and looked upon the job as a settled career. I didn't have the foggiest notion of what I wanted to do except that the shoe business was not for me. Fortunate, in a way, is the man that knows from a young age what he wants to do with his life. It makes for a stabler existence, perhaps, but maybe you miss out on some of the fun of uncertainty.

I re-hooked up with Ray Doherty who was now out of the Navy and attending City College. We did the town a bit though he was married now and on a trajectory that would take him around the world many times in the oil and construction supply business, making him rich along the way. So there was a limit to how much he could participate. We did go to a sawdust-on-the floor beer bar, of the type popular then, called Ole's on Irving Street at 10th Avenue. There he introduced me to some guys he had met in his travels through foster homes and Catholic Social Services institutions. I hadn't met them before but we had a lot in common having spent time in the same foster home orbit, more or less. I had gone to St. Catherines in Benicia which was somewhat the same sort of place as Hanna Center and St. Vincent's where they hailed from. And for a time after my father went broke in the early 50s, we received support from Catholic Social Services as well.

Ole's was to be my principal headquarters for the next several years. I went around to other spots, downtown and in other neighborhoods around town in search of nightlife and girls. Some other young devotees of the neighborhood saloon culture then prevalent in San Francisco tended to hang out in the same joint all the time. I knew this one place in the Mission near where we lived before my mother died, where the clientele graduated from high school right into the corner saloon. They never left it. They couldn't drive, didn't have cars, and hooked up with females very infrequently, if at all. On Sunday afternoon you would find them there, all dressed up in their suits and ties after church, with no place else to go. That was not for me. I may have been headquartered on Irving Street but the entire city was my night-time oyster. (I have since wondered if my mother hadn't died when she did, and I grew up in that neighborhood, whether I would have been sitting at that bar after mass myself.) Biology and society both tell us: "Adapt or die." The dominant alpha male in that group died in Laguna Honda Hospital of alcohol related problems at the age of 50.

The clientele at Ole's tended to work in construction jobs, and until things got rowdier as time went by, it was a good place to meet girls too. It was the typical working class neighborhood saloon life participated in by young men of the time. I did some bay sailing with some guys I met at the bar. And we experimented with the light drugs that were floating around at the time, marijuana and some kind of diet pills, but the idea didn't take with me. I was disturbed quite enough on my own, and alcohol was my drug of choice.

After a time, and at Ray's urging, I think, I enrolled in City College with a major in journalism. I thought I wanted to write. And write I did. In addition to class work, we had to work on the school paper, the *Guardsman*, under the supervision of Joan Nourse, another good woman in my life. I went part time on my job and managed to keep up my night time activities. It wasn't long before my other class work began to suffer.

I remember that as time went on I was writing several articles for each issue of the paper, while classmates who were good at discussing journalism tended not to get in print. I don't know if I was any good but I could produce copy. As part of the job, I had to go about interviewing various members of the faculty and leaders of student organizations. It was then I learned the meaning of the maxim that "work comes to him who will do it." As I talked to student leaders for stories for the paper I found myself being drawn into volunteering to help with the projects in which they were involved. One job I took on was to survey all junior colleges in California by questionnaire to get a statistical profile on each of them, then to compile the data obtained and publish it in book form to be distributed to each contributing school.

It all got to be too much: school life, work life, night life, and extracurricular projects. I'm sure some of it had to do with my aversion to the class room setting. (Later, in the 1970s a tremendous amount of federal money became available to pay police officers to go to school as part of a program to upgrade police departments following the urban meltdown in the 1960s. Golden Gate University established a program at which many of my colleagues went on to earn graduate degrees. I didn't do that. Instead, I studied on my own to scale the promotional ladder from within. I would argue that I stayed and helped run the ship while others went off to school or spent company time working on their class assignments. Maybe it's sour grapes on my part but I don't remember those federal educational programs as having improved institutional performance all that much.)

Back in 1958, I finished the fact book and then chucked it all in. I quit school and I quit my job, and

I went out to the beach at Kelly's Cove with some out-of-work construction guys to intercept girls ("seagulls") on their way to Playland to meet sailors. All I had to live on was the residue of my $110 a month GI school benefit. Several of us shared a little apartment to which my monthly contribution was $10. I was able to scrounge meals from my sisters for a while until they caught on and the word went out. "Kevin doesn't have a job; and he is not looking for one." That put an end to the free meals. More than once, we visited St. Anthony's Dining Room to keep body and spirit together.

Some of the guys I hung with had the unemployment benefit system worked out and knew exactly how long they had to work to accumulate enough benefits so they could take off great swatches of time. I didn't really fit into that scheme so I soon faced the prospect of having to get a job. I have wondered since whether if this had all occurred a few years later, when Great Society benefits became available, whether I would ever have returned to the work force. As it was, my "vacation" lasted only a couple of months. (That is the only period between the age of 15 and my eventual retirement that I was not gainfully employed.)

So, advised of the availability of laboring jobs with the PG&E, I went down and took the test. The work was rigorous but nothing that would challenge the mind. Geary Boulevard was being widened that year and a new gas main was being laid from Masonic Avenue to the beach. I worked as a laborer on the heavy crew that laid the line. I have to say I relished the physical part of it. Others ran from the jackhammer; I took to it with a will. I was in the best shape I had been in since jump school, for all my running around at night.

The PG&E had a career track. The general foreman came out to the job site one day where he approached me and another guy, a U.C. graduate from Lodi who had somehow found himself on the crew, and told us that on the strength of our entry test scores we should take advantage of the track. "You make your living during the day," he said, "and your promotions at night." I had other things to do at night those years and I didn't see myself staying with the company, anyway.

The bogeymen in our household growing up were the "Masons" and the "APAs" (American Protective Association), both non-Catholic organizations who looked out for their own, and according to family lore, had it in for Catholics. I believed that you had to be a Mason to really advance with the company. That may or may not be true but it's what I believed. And I didn't look forward to a life driving around in a truck repairing gas meters. Not that I had anything better in mind.

So, while my SI classmates were finishing up with law school or launching business careers, I dug holes in the morning, and filled them up in the afternoon.

One day at lunch, a fellow worker, a pipefitter, was talking about his several unsuccessful attempts to join the Police Department. He was not giving up, he said, because the pay and benefits were better than he was doing with PG&E, even starting out. He had a better job than I did so I began to think: Why not?

14 – Police Department

Never in my wildest dreams had I ever expected or intended to become a police officer. Many of my friends had wanted the job all their lives. There is a school of thought which holds that those attracted to the police world tend to be rigid moralists who get satisfaction from ordering other people around. There are those, of course, but most I have met came to the job out of feeling of altruism, a desire to help victims of crime, even if that assistance might involve whacking miscreants in the head now and then.

Not only did I not want it. I didn't think that I could measure up to the job. I grew up believing that no matter how fat or old he was any cop could take me out. It was not until I went to City College after my army service, and I sized up the uniformed officers directing traffic there, that I considered the possibility. (I found out later that they were not regular officers at all but students in the Police Science course, most of whom would never qualify for the regular department.)

I went to City Hall after work one day and picked up an application. And one sunny Saturday morning soon thereafter, I went with several hundred others to Mission High School where we took the written examination. When those results came in, those of us who passed the written went to the Polo Field in Golden Gate Park where we took the physical part of the examination which consisted of doing a certain number of pull-ups (or overhead one-armed presses with a 50 pound dumbbell), vaulting a horse, and running 220 yards on the track in a given number of seconds. The medical examination followed. And there was also a background investigation involving interviews with neighbors and merchants near where the candidate lived. All-in-all it was a pretty cut-and-dried, objective process.

I found out later that the selection process hadn't always been so straightforward. Before the introduction of Civil Service at the turn of the twentieth century, appointment had been under the direct control of the Police Commission. Several late nineteenth-century scandals, which revealed that police appointments could be bought for several hundred dollars, brought about the introduction of Civil Service reforms in the 1900 Charter. Henceforth, entry-level and promotional jobs in the police department –except for a few exempt positions at the top—were to be awarded on the basis of competitive written objective examinations. That's the way the process would work for the better part of the century.

On July 1, 1959 I was appointed to the San Francisco Police Department and assigned to the then Police Academy at 37th and Fulton for recruit training. The single most powerful impression I retain from that period is the feeling of all-enveloping welcome that embraced me on joining the department. It was the men.

Figure 13-Swearing In July 1, 1959

Old San Franciscans look back on the time "Before the War" when the city was a magic place. It really was. Immediately following the 1906 Earthquake and Fire, almost half the city's population departed. Many returned later; some did not. The latter were replaced by a large influx of workingmen, mostly from Europe, who came to rebuild the fallen city. Further immigration was greatly curtailed by World War One, and more still by the restrictive immigration legislation of the 1920s. San Franciscans of different backgrounds were given time to assimilate with one another. Chinatown always excepted (and much of that was self-imposed), there were no strictly enforced ethnic or racial ghettoes in San Francisco such as had grown up in other cities.

Surrounded on three sides by water and insulated by a continent from the industrial stinkpots of the East, San Francisco stood serene, a model of amity to which others could aspire. That is not to say the city was an ethnic and racial paradise. Ed Cassidy told me of going from the Mission to a dance at Fugazi Hall in North Beach in the late 1930s and being made feel unwelcome by young Italians there.

And it was evident to me, even at a very early age, that black people were somehow different. My first experience with a black person was in about 1939 with the son of our mailman at 570 30th Street. The boy was referred to in our household, in the usage of the time, as "George Washington the nigger boy." I do remember an undercurrent of concern evinced by my parents because he played with my sister. Compared to just about every place else, though, such bigotry as existed in pre-War San Francisco was relatively benign. George Washington was our neighbor, after all; he didn't live in some faraway ghetto.

It really was a small town then. Once during the War, when the German lady who owned the big apartment house at the top of Collingwood Street complained we were trespassing on her property, (we had convinced ourselves that she was harboring Nazis) the call to "knock it off" came directly from the Mayor's Office, and they knew who we were by name. All in all, the city was a special place, and the men who inducted me into the police department—many if not most of them Irish American—had been raised in that special world. They had been young boys during the Depression 30's and then gone off to fight the Second World War. They then returned home to take wives and start raising families. They were not perfect; they were products of the values of their time, even as most of us are captives of our own. There were some rough-edged characters among them but for the most part they were "gentlemen," as the term was defined at the time.

My comfort level doubtless came naturally enough. San Francisco's Irish community had a large say in how things went in those days, and I had all the necessary San Francisco credentials at the time. But unbeknownst to us, the old San Francisco had already begun to change. Over successive years, newcomers from other, harsher climes would arrive in San Francisco and supplant the gentler natives from their leading positions in San Francisco's world.

The police academy training lasted sixteen weeks. Today, large numbers of police candidates are eliminated in the training process. Then, if you made the cut and got in, you were more or less a member of the club, and you had to foul up very badly to be thrown out. The course work consisted mainly of lectures by old-timers who recounted their exploits from years on the job. I remember one lieutenant who told of how he was hitting a man once and the man wouldn't fall down. He then learned that the man's coat had been hooked to the wall behind, preventing him from falling. I suppose the lesson there was to make sure your man was not hanging from a hook when you go to knock him down.

I did learn one thing of practical utility, though I never had to use it on the street. Ed Epting, our physical instructor at the academy, showed us how to disarm a man with a gun pointing at your stomach. The feat involves striking the barrel of your opponent's pistol with your left hand while hitting his wrist from the other side with your right. It works. I've tried it with friends and empty pistols over the years and invariably was able to get the gun away from them. I'd bet I could do it still.

But for the most part we didn't learn much of practical importance, at least in the Academy itself. On Friday nights, we donned our brand new uniforms, strapped on our brand new revolvers and were assigned with regular patrol officers in the stations to get a taste of the street. One night I was assigned with Officer Jim Shannon (later deputy chief) to his patrol car in the Mission. A 415 call came in for the Army Street projects. I knew what a 415 call was—a fight or disturbance. I remember thinking, as we headed to the address, that we were expected to get out of the car and just start fighting. I had no particular desire to fight like that but if that is what the job called for, I was ready to do it. As things turned out, it was some black woman railing at her husband for buying nylon stockings for a woman in a bar on Fillmore Street. Jim Shannon separated them and we all went our merry ways.

They also taught us about police reports at the Academy, using a large blow-up of a report form. The instructor pointed to the various boxes on the form telling us what to put where. I never did figure out in the Academy what that was all about. Once on the street, however, it all became obvious: fill in the boxes with administrative data as necessary, and then write a little story about what the reportee/victim had to say. When I entered the

Academy, I weighed 184 pounds, fit from all the heavy labor. By graduation I had ballooned to a reasonably fit 220, thanks to the morning pre-class sessions with coffee and donuts, and the mostly sedentary classroom life, interrupted only by a modicum of PT and work on the mats.

After graduation from the Academy, we were sent to district stations. (The plan then was to spend one year each in two district stations before settling in finally to a third.) My first station was Northern, then located at 841 Ellis, between Van Ness and Polk. Then, as now, the district encompassed the area from Civic Center and the Upper Tenderloin, over to the Fillmore District and parts of Pacific Heights.

Following the mandatory break-in period on "the book," fielding phoned requests from citizens for help and entering information in the big log book and calls from officers into the ring-in book, we finally made it to the street. The district was going through "Redevelopment" at the time and many Western Addition Victorians were in the process of being torn down. This gave rise to a class of "Redevelopment" burglars who looted the abandoned buildings for copper pipes and other saleable salvage. I couldn't help but notice that many of the young black guys we arrested were not locally born. Many hailed from Texas and Louisiana as I recall.

Fillmore Street itself, between McAllister and Geary, had yet to be redeveloped and had much of its old flavor. There was a racial mix of bars and other businesses, black and white, unlike the almost exclusively black complexion of later years. There were two competing supermarkets, a Safeway and something else, opposite each other on the corner of Fillmore and Turk, where Northern Station stands today.

It was exciting to be out and about, and on the prowl at night. I suppose new officers feel that same way today. As a 4/12 watch came to an end, I would hope that something big would go down to keep us over for the next watch. I began to see a San Francisco I didn't know from a perspective of which I had never been aware. They had told us at the Academy that as we went along in the department the number of our non-police friends would decline. It was the crazy hours, they said, which would cause us to drift apart. There was more to it than that. I had entered a world of human misery that many of my friends would not understand, and whose gallows humor they would not get.

It was while I was at Northern Station that the department got a preview of things to come. In May 1960, the House Un-American Activities Committee (HUAC), then in the full flush of its heyday, began to conduct hearings in the Board of Supervisors Chambers in City Hall. The committee handed out admission cards to organizations friendly to its work, thus excluding others. The proceedings began on May 12 and a number of Bay Area students who had shown up to protest the proceedings found themselves excluded. The next day the students showed up in force and vocally protested their exclusion. Courts adjourned because the noise level of the protestors made it impossible to proceed. Finally, violence between police and demonstrators erupted at the police barricades and the nominal officer-in-charge, a detective assigned to the Intelligence Unit, ordered the nearby fire hoses deployed and washed the protesting demonstrators down the inside steps of City Hall. A riot call went out and in all 64, mostly students from Berkeley, were arrested and carted off to jail.

Sixty-three of the arrestees were promptly released, all except Robert Meisenback, the 22 year old student who, police charged, precipitated the riot by jumping the police barricade and striking a police officer with his own club. At his trial the next year, the defense produced a *Chronicle* photograph showing Meisenback in the background calmly smoking a pipe as students were washed down the stairs. He was promptly acquitted. It's conceivable, though unlikely, that some other student had in fact started the melee by jumping over the barricade and that in the confusion police grabbed the wrong man. Northern Station officers didn't take much guff in those days.

There are other factors which call police operations that day into question. Why, on the second day of demonstrations, were 55 police officers assigned to a crowd control situation without any supervisory or command officers, but under the nominal supervision of a non-supervisory detective? The department had not faced any kind of riotous conduct since the VJ-Day disorders in 1945 and was simply unprepared to deal with crowd situations, a phenomenon which was to recur frequently in following years. What comes through when one examines the record a half century after the event is the extent to which press and public almost unanimously supported the police actions taken that day. It was a very different world, indeed, from that which was on its way.

After a year at Northern I was sent to Central Station, "the big A," then next to the old Hall of Justice, on Washington between Kearny and Montgomery. The district ran from the North side of Market and along Leavenworth to the Bay on the North and East. Included in its jurisdiction were the Tenderloin, Nob Hill, the Financial District and Chinatown and North Beach. Anything could happen there, and it often did.

The Tenderloin had a distinct Runyonesque flavor, with a lot of Nathan Detroit wannabes standing around with cigars in one corner of their mouths while they talked out of the other. I don't remember worrying about being in any special danger. It was my first introduction to Chinatown too. When assigned to inside duty on "the book" on the midnight watch during the customary break-in period, we would walk up to the Sai Yon Café for breakfast at our 3 am break. The restaurant would be full with Chinese families, including small children, who had just gotten off work in factories.

When you got "off the book" you would be assigned as a floater to work among the various radio cars with the regular men in various parts of the district. Each day you would have to check the board to see your assignment for the next day and find out if your assignment was to and "early" or "late" car. I did this for a time but I didn't like all the uncertainty so when a vacancy occurred on the three-wheel motorcycle I put in for it and was accepted.

The basic job of the three-wheeler was to answer district calls about autos blocking driveways and other traffic offenses. On that assignment I had the run of the district and no midnight watches. The job was mainly traffic but you were expected also to respond to general emergency calls. Once at a fire, I was the only vehicle able to get down a narrow congested alley on Telegraph Hill, and was thus the only one available to rescue an invalid woman from her upstairs apartment. The sergeant put me in for a meritorious award on that one but the captain said there since there was no press coverage he wouldn't pass it along. I later relinquished my three-wheeler job to a man who needed to be off midnights so he could nurse his ailing mother, and I took a job on the patrol wagon with Herman Rossback. My job was on the back where the chief skill set required was the ability to command, charm or wrestle drunks into the wagon.

An inherent feature of the police job in the public mind is the bond that exists between two partners, forged by their shared and adversity in the dangerous street world they inhabit. Ask just about any police officer and he can name his steady partner or partners. Not me. As I look back on the time, I realize that for the most part in almost all the jobs I've had, I worked by myself. There were many friends and co-workers, of course, who would and did back me up, but with the exception of Herman Rossback, on the wagon at Central, there was never anyone, I could say, who would be my radio car or foot beat partner from day-to-day.

After two years at busy downtown stations I was sent to the relatively law-abiding Richmond, where I would spend the next five years. "Everything happens at the Richmond," Inspector "Yash" Yasinitsky told me once. "It just doesn't happen as often." I sometimes wondered if I was sent to a less active station because of my performance downtown. I had handled everything that came to me—walked down the same bad alleys as much as anybody else. But by no stretch of the imagination can I be said to have been one of those super-active officers who seek out trouble and don't let anything get by.

I had a problem with hypocrisy. My own. Having been less than a model citizen myself, I felt constrained about coming down too hard on people doing much as I had done. That is not to say that I let everything go by. If someone was hurting someone else I would step in, and I had no moral reservations about arresting burglars or people with guns. But I found it more difficult to get fired up about the sumptuary laws, where no one was obviously being hurt. Later, I came to see that commercial vice conditions had to be suppressed or they would poison a neighborhood, but as a young officer I preferred to concentrate on other duties.

My first regular assignment at Richmond Station was as operator of one of the four one-man radio cars. My sector, Radio One, covered the area from Presidio Avenue to Arguello between Fulton Street and the Presidio Wall. The sergeants all worked on foot in those days, which left us largely unsupervised. Indeed, on those occasional instances when a sergeant showed up on the scene, I would feel insulted when he tried to intervene. We did it ninety-five percent of the time, I reasoned, and we didn't need him now.

I didn't realize it at the time but my sector covered the very streets where my grandfather, Humphrey, had grown up as a young boy. Because my mother died before I could talk to her about it, it was only much later that I was able to research that side of the family. Thus I don't now much about my grandfather as a child. But I'm fairly sure I know where he was on November 14, 1874. That was the date of the inauguration of the Bay District Race track just down Point Lobos Road (Geary Boulevard) from Collins Street where the family lived. The track, between First Avenue (Arguello) and Fifth, hosted a race that day with the biggest purse in racing history. It was the biggest event to occur in that then sparsely settled part of the city and I can't conceive of a neighborhood 9-year old who would not be conscious of the endless stream of sportsmen heading out the toll road to the track or perched on Lone Mountain just behind his house to watch the race. Two even sat atop the cross at the mountain's peak.

I have a pretty good idea where he was on November 7, 1878 as well. That was the day that

Ann Barry was raped, mutilated and murdered in her home on Parker Street just opposite the present site of St. Ignatius Church and just a few blocks away from his home. Any self respecting neighborhood 13-year old would have surely been attracted to the scene. The murder inspired a massive manhunt of the area by the entire police detective force and a detachment of mounted soldiers from the Presidio who quartered the area looking for the suspect. The killer was indentified as Daniel "Red Mike" Sullivan who worked at the Masonic Cemetery just across the street from the crime scene. Sullivan was known to frequent the Barbary Coast so cemetery workers who knew him were teamed up with police officers and patrolled the downtown area. (My great-grandfather, Denis, was likely one of the searchers.) It was there Sullivan was captured by one of his fellow workers. By the time I worked the radio car sector, the original family dwelling on the corner of Collins and Geary had been replaced by a low-rent drive-in restaurant. The family's late nineteenth century residence remains, however—the three story flats across the street next to the carwash.

One thing I and other retired officers have noticed is the tendency of officers these days to pull their firearms. It's a matter of "officer safety" I'm informed, along with swarming techniques and spreading suspects on the ground. It must be working because the per capita incidence of officers shot in the line of duty has gone down. In those days there was a stigma attached to those who pulled their guns too readily. The thinking was that once you pointed it at someone the only options remaining were to shoot them or put it back away, like Barney Fife. You might pull it out on iffy calls, and hold it along your leg, but there was less waving guns around than is now apparently the case.

It was the same thing with back-ups. The traditions harked back to a time when officers all worked alone and on foot without communications to headquarters or each other. With one-man cars, we would automatically fill in on each other for dangerous sounding calls, but if you called yourself for assistance you would hear a disembodied voice on the police channel: "What's the matter? Can't you handle it?"

Bill Keays (later deputy chief) told how in the late 1930s he was walking a beat on lower Mission Street when he got in a fight with a crazy man. He was relieved, he said, to see the officer on the adjoining beat approaching. As he tumbled around with his adversary he noticed that the senior officer had stopped across the street and watched the fight. After Keays had subdued him man by himself, he asked the older officer why he hadn't come to his aid. "I would have intervened if it looked as though you were losing," said the other officer, "but you are going to be alone most of the time and you have to be able to handle things by yourself.

A common call, on weekend nights particularly, had to do with working-men husbands coming home drunk. You would arrive on the scene to find the drunken husband and the irate wife, with perhaps a few children peering sheepishly around the corner. She wanted him out and it was your job to get him out. You could try to arrest him on the spot which would have humiliated him in front of his wife and children and very likely result in a traumatic fight. So, more than once I charmed the suspect in, driving him unsearched in the passenger seat of the radio car next to me to the station where the Sergeant would "straighten things out with his wife." Once in the station, the rules would change. Over the years, such practices got officers killed. But that's what we did.

After a year or so in the car, I was assigned to a foot beat on outer Geary and Clement, between 14th and 32nd. It was pleasant enough and undemanding duty. On the evening shift most of the work had to do with merchants on the beat, particularly the bars, some of which had more trouble than others. I recently took a ride along my old beat and counted the places that had on-sale liquor licenses. In my time there were 22; today there are eight. We switched back and forth weekly 4 pm to 12 pm shifts to midnight watches which ran from midnight to 8 am. Aside from the fact that it is probably the least healthful way of organizing shift work, I soon realized even then that it was a ridiculous waste of manpower walking around on the midnights. But I didn't complain. Neither did I do much to advance the cause of justice though I might have prevented a bit of crime by my very presence.

Most of the businesses closed down on the midnight watch except for the bars and a few all-night restaurants, and that's where the foot beat men found themselves in the small hours of the morning. To be honest, some napped, but I wasn't at ease enough in uniform to allow myself to be so vulnerable. Often, instead, I would sit in the well-lighted all-night Laundromat at 15th and Geary reading books.

While on the evening watch, I met and became friends with one particular merchant on the beat, Fred Hill, at his Canterbury Corner Book Store at 17th and Geary. One day, in uniform, I was discussing some book or other with him when I noticed a woman customer watching me with a look of apparent puzzlement. I asked her if I could help her and she said, with a note of disbelief in her voice, "A policeman who reads?" I'm not always ready with the instant mot, but that I time I didn't miss a beat. "Some of us can," I said to her "and we tell the others."

She had apparently not gotten the bulletin that we are not supposed to stereotype people. Still, her surprise was understandable for, truth to be told, as with many stereotypes, this one contains a kernel of truth. Those attracted to police work, at least in those days, tended more to be men of action than men of the reflective type. That is not to say that they were necessarily less than bright. We have learned recently of more and different "intelligences" than those measured by verbal and mathematical tests. While I may have read more than most, I have met many officers at all ranks who didn't read much at all, and who were far superior to me in investigative and human relations skills.

"When constabulary's work's to be done," we generally want someone who will *act* in our behalf.

Part of the beat man's job involved psychological legerdemain. On foot and out of radio contact, you were even farther from any possible assistance. When I later moved to Marin County and looked at the police beat section of the local paper I was amazed at the number of arrests from one of the few bars in town. Invariably the charge would be giving false information to a police officer and resisting arrest. I concluded that the Novato police just didn't understand the niceties of the saloon/police relationship. For one thing, as with the drunken husband in his kitchen on Friday night, you don't come on too strong and humiliate a man in front of his friends unnecessarily or you will force him to resist.

One device is to create an environment in which arrestees thought any resistance would be hopeless. An old-timer once told me how he had been broken in. His instructor told him that when he got a beat, to go to the roughest bar on the beat. It's all relative but every beat has one. Then, his instructor said. "Pick out someone you can beat and do so." The idea was that the legend of your prowess would spread to the saloon community and thereafter its denizens would treat you with respect.

Things were not that wild when I got the beat but I did once observe the legend creation phenomenon at work on my behalf. One of my self-assigned duties on the midnight watch was to monitor the activities at the Flying Saucer, an all night restaurant then at the corner of 27th and Geary, where the outpourings of the bars around town would end up after the 2 am closings for breakfast. Loaded as the place was with drunks, it sometimes made for interesting duty. One St. Patrick's night I was at my station by the cash register and I could see that I was in for it. One patron was sitting there calmly wearing a business suit with collar and tie but somehow or other his shirt was gone, doubtless having been detached in some adventure elsewhere in town.

Two sailors in civilian clothes started acting up so I called the district car to take them to the station. As I put one in the back seat, he opened the other rear door and went out the other side (no back door locks in those days). I went around to put him back in, and in the ensuing struggle our weight sprung the rear door which had been hanging open. A waitress in the restaurant saw my hat fly off and placed an "officer-needs-assistance" call. That brought the cavalry, with Frank Williams leading the charge, and when the drunks poured out of the restaurant the festivities began. By the time the story got down to the Gold Chips Bar at the other end of the beat the next day, it went that I had thrown the sailor into the back seat so hard that it sprung open the closed rear door. An impossibility of course but I didn't disabuse them of that fact. They wanted to believe.

But all was not work. We had a key to the Rossi Playground pool and sometimes we would go for midnight swims, joined on occasion by compliant night waitresses from district restaurants. There were also the runs around the Polo Field in Golden

Gate Park and working out on the mats. I bought a bicycle and explored the city on two wheels. Like the Southern Pacific I learned to get around the hills. Once a friend of mine and I rode from the rear of Richmond Station down along the Coast Highway to Los Angeles.

But much or our off-duty socialization took place in district's bars. Non-shift workers don't really understand. People who work days and get home at 6 pm or so have time to decompress before retiring for the night. When you get off at midnight, particularly after an exciting day, you want to unwind. That's what we did--some of us—assembling in local bars, where we would debrief until 2 am closing time. Sometimes we lost track of the time.

The drinking. From its earliest founding, San Francisco was a drinking town and we were a San Francisco institution, the oldest city department in fact. In the days before the proliferation of automobiles, according to accounts of the time, half the town walked around drunk. There was an afternoon tradition in the Financial District dubbed "seeing the elephant" in which downtown businessmen would drink from bar to bar up one side of Kearny Street and down the other. The police department was always the last to let go of old traditions. There are humorous stories about stunts pulled by officers when in their cups, but in the end, their life stories almost always end on sad note.

I did my share of drinking, and perhaps more, but I restricted my activities almost exclusively to off-duty times. Very early on, I noticed some day-watch officers walking around in a perpetual state of maintenance inebriation. I reasoned that they had picked up and ingrained those habits by accepting the free drinks offered when they worked nights. Barkeepers were always willing to give officers free drinks to keep on their good side. So I made it my plan not to participate in the hours long pre-prandial sessions that some officers indulged in on the 4/12 watch. I reserved my sport for when I got off.

15 – Getting Serious

The 1960s's and early 1970s was a period of civil rights demonstrations and countless marches against the Vietnam War. It was also a period that saw our inner cities burn, and crime figures climb up the charts, while flower children took to drugs and danced in the streets. It seemed that an entire post-war generation had repudiated its parents' values and snubbed its nose at everything held sacred in the past. The police, wherever they were situated, were ineluctably drawn into the unfolding events.

The bellwether event in the rising crime rate to our minds was the April Aaron case. One evening in May 1962 a young black man, dubbed "the Slasher" by the press at the time, badly cut a young Latter Day Saints woman named April Aaron as she walked through the Panhandle on her way to a church dance. The press went nuts and the department mobilized to catch the vicious criminal. A great deal of racial profiling went on, I suppose, without much noticeable complaint.

The halcyon days had actually come to an end years earlier. In a series titled "Terror in the Streets" in 1958, *Chronicle* reporter Art Hoppe reported that statistically it was twice as dangerous to walk the streets of San Francisco as it had been before World War II. One of the most dangerous areas cited was the largely black Fillmore District. But then as now, the paper danced around the issue of racial crime.

"One of those areas is predominately Negro," Hoppe wrote "and the criminals are Negro as well. But this growing violence in San Francisco is not confined to Negro areas. All slum areas have a high incidence of crime on the streets."

The fact of the matter is that a disproportionate amount of the increasing street violence was committed by young black males. (I am not going to produce a sociological treatise on the causes of minority crime in what is a personal memoir, except to say that the undeniable reality of who was committing a disproportionate amount of violent crime inevitably shaped police attitudes about how we perceived different people. I have written extensively on the topic elsewhere[1])

For the first half of the 1960s, I remained assigned to Richmond Station, away from the center of events but some of it found us there. There was the picketing and the sit-in at Mel's Drive-In in 1963, at which the officer toting Terrence Hallinan away lost his grip and dropped the protesting attorney on his head. There was no one important present to take note of anything because the District Captain and Supervising Captain had departed from the scene before the arrests began, a common practice at the time. Supervisor Terry Francois showed up to make a nominal showing for the demonstrators before departing himself.

When conditions called for it at major events, we would be detailed to help out downtown. That's

---

[1] See my *Dangerous Strangers: Minority Newcomers and Criminal Violence in the Urban West.* (New York: Palgrave-MacMillan, 2005.)

how I ended up at the Auto Row Sit-in on Van Ness. All was confusion and I remember a lieutenant instructing us not to make any arrests unless someone of at least the rank of lieutenant was present. Then the lieutenant left.

I didn't bear the demonstrators any particular animus though I can't say the same for them. I remember one pretty co-ed at Chrysler who was pouring venom my way. I told her that I would rather be elsewhere that day picking up my new bicycle. I guess I touched her on the human level because immediately her manner softened. If the setting had been different, maybe. . .

We also made the Hunter's Point Riot in 1966. It all started on the afternoon of September 27—in the midst of the annual "Indian Summer" warm spell—over a police shooting of a young black man, and ran over to the next day. It wasn't much by the standards of other 60's urban riots but it was more than we had been accustomed to in recent times. There was a companion disturbance in the Fillmore the same night. I was at home when the call came in to report to duty and I remember my chief reaction as being excited that we were going to see some real action.

They gathered us up in the Richmond, staged us at Park Station and then moved us out to Third Street where I remember a group of us chasing some black kids over the hills, and directing traffic on Third Street as morning began to arrive. A group of middle-aged black women, all dressed in white (beauty parlor workers, I think) encouraged us to give those boys "what for" for keeping them away from their jobs.

A year earlier when Watts erupted into violence leaving 34 dead, 1100 injured and $100 million in property damage, I had looked into it. I picked up *Rivers of Blood, Years of Darkness,* an account of the Los Angeles riot. From the book I learned that the Los Angeles police officers had put their riot procedures into effect but that the procedures hadn't worked. I remember thinking at the time that we didn't have any riot procedures at all.

During the same period, San Francisco's Haight Ashbury District became the focal point of what became known as the "Summer of Love." Thousands upon thousands of young people, many runaways in their teens, streamed into San Francisco from all over the nation in answer to Timothy Leary's invitation to "tune in, turn on and drop out." The pimps and drug dealers were waiting for them, and in the end many of the kids were in fact "turned out," as prostitutes and worse.

Each Sunday, the crowds would take over Haight Street and turn it into an open-air drug and music market. And just as regularly we would show up and clear the streets. The smell of tear gas was a perennial bouquet. I didn't think about it at the time, but the day-watch officers at Park Station—the men who bore the brunt of the duty those summers—would have been the same older men who had lived through the depression and fought the World War, only to see their own children's' contemporaries ridicule everything they held dear. No wonder they were pissed off.

It was in the mid-1960's that I finally began to get serious about things, and just in time, because my world was becoming a more serious place. I can thank Jeannie in large part for my conversion. In late 1964 I escorted my sister Sheila to a party on Castro Street she wanted to attend. There I met two young girls, Judy and Jeannie, roommates who lived at 1290 Grove Street, at Divisadero. I became engaged in a conversation with Judy who was writing a college paper discussing "The Rights of the minority and the will of the majority." I suggested a couple of books that might help her and offered to take them by the next day. (One of them was Faulkner's *Intruder in the Dust.* The other one I can't remember.) I showed up at Grove Street the next afternoon with the books in hand. Judy was out someplace else so Jeannie and I talked. We discussed alligators. She was my choice anyway.

We were married at Saint Monica's Church at 23rd and Geary on February 13, 1965. Jeannie was an orphan girl from a good family so we did the wedding pretty much on our own. We had the wedding breakfast in a rib joint on Divisadero Street. It was the kind of place where the proprietress locked and unlocked the cash register at each transaction to make sure the patrons at that end of the counter didn't run off with its contents. I supplanted Judy at Grove Street for while.

As a married man, I had to change my ways. I could no longer maintain the social life that had been mine the whole of my adult life. So, with some free time on my hands I read more and began to think about things. I read generally but with a focus on the criminal justice history of old San Francisco, a subject which had interested me for some time. And I began to set my thoughts down on paper, perhaps recognizing on some level that this memoir's day would come

Divisadero at Grove was a mixed race neighborhood at the time and everybody seemed to have been getting along. But racial tensions were increasing. My first experience with such tension had been in 1952 when a high school classmate and his older brother were confronted by a group of African-American boys in front of Kezar Pavilion. At that time it was truly an exceptional event. But things were changing. Every year, just before football season commenced, the city's high schools conducted a Pageant at Kezar Stadium during which the various schools would play one quarter of football against each other. The event was suspended after 1956 because at the Pageant that year groups of young blacks had gone about the stands assaulting whites.

I'd have to say I was pretty liberal at the time, having inhaled the ideas of Jack London and Upton Sinclair among others in my autodidactic pursuit of knowledge. (I once subscribed to the United World Federalist magazine.) But my ideas had begun to shift in the crucible of reality. One time, Jeannie was present in the neighborhood laundromat when two black men fought it out with knives. Once a group of young black boys accosted her walking our

Samoyed, Trishka, at Alamo Square. A frightened Trishka—her sled dog instincts clicking in—pulled Jeannie up a steep incline at the leash's end, where the boys could not follow. Each night at work I listened on the police radio to the calls of violence near our home.

My father joined us for dinner on Grove Street one night and related how he had once had black customers in the neighborhood, who he had to abandon because of thuggish behavior by young men in the area. The angry looks on the faces of the young black men were identical, he said, to the looks of some young Irishmen of his own youth, "who thought that killing an Englishman would assure their entry into heaven."

In October Jeannie and I bought our first house, at 1225 Skyline Drive in Daly City. I was the first of my immediate family to move outside of San Francisco since the 1860s. There was a strong economic incentive to leave the city. Across the line, we could buy the same house as in the city, only new, and at half the price.

As I look at it now, much of the self-exploratory writing I did then consists of the puerile maunderings of an immature searcher, trying to figure out his confused world. One entry, that for October 10, 1965, however—when we were about to move to Daly City—while of no particular literary merit, does accurately reflect my feelings at the time:

In our neighborhood there are many who have been hurt. They respond to that hurt by accosting my wife on her way to the park. She hasn't wounded anyone, yet they subject her to their obscene proposals. I notice the hurt in their glares perhaps because in my work I come in contact with the wounded ones. Anyway, we are leaving this place to the wounded and hurt, and we are going to a place where people will allow us to raise our children without fear of reprisal for something we didn't cause in the first place. I chose not to sacrifice my generation and the next one to the healing of the wounds of humanity.

We moved to Daly City and our son, Davitt, was born on December 18th 1965. I can see him now in my mind's eye, sleeping serenely wrapped up in his yellow blanket, his little widow-peaked head sticking out, while all around him red faced babies screamed at the gods. (I had stopped smoking some years earlier, and as I handed out cigars celebrating his birth, I became hooked again and didn't quit for good until 1980.)

I had never thought much before about the prospect of promotion. The tests had come and gone and I let them go. But now, with a family to feed and a mortgage to pay, I began to get some ambition, and to look beyond my own immediate selfish needs. There were two ways to get ahead at the time. You could get assigned to the detective bureau (Inspectors) through good investigative street work or political juice. The other was to pass the promotional test for Sergeant and then on up. I didn't know anybody politically and I hadn't made any great record of arrests, so I chose the latter way to go.

I had an edge, I suppose, because I was used to reading a lot, and many of my colleagues weren't. It was mainly a matter of directing my reading toward the technical matters on which we would be tested. But there was more to it than that. Points on the final score were awarded for seniority (up to 15 percent) and military veteran's preference (three percent) which gave older officers a boost. The test itself was more an obstacle course than it was a measure of intelligence or aptitude. It rewarded those who took the time—and it did take a lot of time—to master the arcana of the various subjects in the scope of books: investigations, management, supervision, personnel matters, law, ordinances and the department rules. It seems I tested well.

Figure 14-New Sergeants. "The kid" center rear.

In July 1967, I was promoted to the rank of sergeant and transferred to Central Station, by now moved to 2475 Greenwich Street while the new Central Station on Vallejo Street was being erected. New sergeants, like patrolmen, had to serve their time "on the book." When the next new sergeant came along, though, I was out on the street, in a car by myself, supervising the officers assigned to radio sector patrols. I noticed that the district had changed. For one thing, the Tenderloin had deteriorated. The most visible manifestation of change was the appearance of many new black faces, and a new aura of fear. For all its seediness before, the Tenderloin head been a relatively safe place. It was peopled largely by older white pensioners and seamen who lived in the cheap residential hotels and frequented the low end bars. (As part of the research for another book I came to the realization that these people were being murdered out of the neighborhood. The numbers weren't such that we noticed any particular wave in progress. But when you took a longer look, you noticed a lot of old seamen killed in the street in apparent robberies and older women killed in their rooms, presumably by unknown suspects. By extrapolating from the race of the suspects in the few cases in which arrests were made, it is fair to conclude that we had a low-intensity ethnic cleansing going on in the Tenderloin in those years. Black on white.)

What had occurred was that when the Fillmore District had been torn down for Redevelopment, many black families had moved to Bayview and

Hunters Point. The street characters, who had worked Fillmore Street before, moved down into the Tenderloin. Damon Runyon types were still around but the climate had changed to closer to what it is today.

The demonstrations continued as they would until the end of the Vietnam War. For a time, I was assigned to the day watch, supervising a squad of officers. Our duty was to patrol the district during the day, subject to calls from State College which was then undergoing daily demonstrations in 1968. Several times we were called out there to support the regular forces assigned. For several months along in this period we had no days off. I had always thought I could work that way with no ill effects. I was wrong.

It's not just the physical toll. Everyone who works the street in uniform, no matter where, is constantly subjected to a continuous low-grade level of psychic stress. It's not so much about what is for sure to happen; it's what might happen when you go in on any kind of call. Someplace in the back of your mind is the prospect that you are going to walk into a bullet. It doesn't happen all that often, but the thought is always there.

In the normal course of affairs we would work five days, then be relieved for two. As you neared the fifth day, as I came to realize, the stress level would grow. It would diminish on your two days off and you would return with batteries charged to begin the cycle again. But with no days off for weeks and months on end, the psychic stress would accumulate. I got through it OK but I also realized that I was not as indestructible as I had thought. It *is* a different kind of job.

16 - Downtown

I had hardly made sergeant when the test for lieutenant was announced. Because of the seniority points given to older officers, common wisdom had it that the odds were against my passing. But the books being used were almost the same as those I had most diligently studied for the sergeant's examination, so I took a flyer and passed high enough to expect an early appointment.

In the meantime, the fog-shrouded Westlake summers didn't suit my wife and son, so we moved to Marin County, to Novato, where many city workers had found homes. On April 10, 1968 our darling Christine was born.

I worked for a time as an acting lieutenant and then in February 1970 Chief Thomas Cahill retired and was replaced by Al Nelder. The retirements occasioned by the selection of the new chief shook loose enough positions so that on February 13, I was sworn in as a regular lieutenant.

Nelder's replacement of Cahill was more than a simple administrative shift. It amounted to an ethno-religious changing of the guard. It appears that Chief Nelder was highly suspicious of the largely Irish Catholic members of the Fatima Society, many of whom had positions around the Hall of Justice. Frank Jordan, later Chief of Police and Mayor, was removed from his job answering phones in the chief's office to Park Station. Sergeant Jack Young was transferred to Ingleside Station where he was murdered a year later by the Black Liberation Army. Chief Nelder's appointments to exempt positions were almost universally not Irish Catholic.

Figure 15-The New Lieutenant.

On my appointment, I was sent temporarily to Richmond Station as a night watch platoon commander because there was no permanent hole for me to fill. That very night—and just one station over—radicals bombed Park Station, killing Sergeant Brian McDonnell, and wounding several other officers severely.

The new chief responded to the scene and I remember his first order, transmitted over the police radio: "Check the nearby saloons." Now that was a good technique to catch downtown bank robbers in the 1950's because that's where robbers—usually not the sharpest knives in the drawer—often headed to enjoy their newfound wealth. But anyone aware of the social upheaval we were going through in the 1970's should have known that the kind of people who blew up police stations were not going to head for the Kezar Club on Stanyan Street to celebrate. I wondered if we were up to the task at hand.

It was a dangerous time to be a police officer in San Francisco, or any big city for that matter. Fourteen San Francisco police officers were murdered in the line of duty between 1965 and 1975, the deadliest decade in the department's history. There is one aspect of police killing in more recent times that didn't occur in earlier years. Since the late 1960s a number of officers have been the victim of out-and-out assassinations. First was Officer Herman George, shot by rifle fire as he sat in the Housing Police office. Sergeant Brian McDonnell was killed in the terrorist bombing of Park Police Station in 1970 and Officer Richard Radetich was assassinated on Waller Street a few months later. In 1971 Sergeant Jack Young was murdered in an armed invasion of Ingleside Station by the Black Liberation Army (BLA) as part of a nationwide campaign to kill police officers. (Today, as his killers are finally being brought to justice there is groundswell of official and "community" support to forgive and forget. Others may forget but you can bet that that Sergeant Young's fellow officers will not abandon his memory). The next year Officer Code Beverly was shot and killed by a sniper on Valencia street as he walked to his beat.

In recent years, the number of officers murdered in the line of duty has gone down appreciatively. The declines are usually explained by the introduction of soft body armor into the arsenal of police defensive equipment, and improved training in police practices. Some old timers have been known to wonder at the tendency of modern officers to draw their weapons so freely and their vigorous spreading people, "putting them on the ground" and cuffing them, even for minor crimes. That same concern has been expressed by community groups who sometimes see police practices as invasive and heavy handed. But when one looks at the number of officers who were killed in times past for failing to exercise adequate officer safety techniques over the century and a half, and the marked decline in officers' deaths since such techniques have been implemented, the aggressive tactics might just be a price that society has to pay. Otherwise, as a *Chronicle* editor warned in 1878 in a similar context, "no officer who has a wife and family could be blamed for keeping out of the way of danger."

Shortly thereafter I was assigned for a few months as officer-in-charge of the General Work Detail as a relief for the regular man who was absent on sick leave. The Homicide Detail had responsibility for Sergeant McDonnell's killing. The bombing was ours. Next I was sent to Patrol Headquarters, then under the command of Supervising Captain Jeremiah Taylor, who kept me on as a member of his staff. I had always worked out of stations before, and the Hall of Justice was one big mystery to me. We in the stations had a vague idea that maybe half the department worked out of the

Hall of Justice but what they were all up to we did not know.

At the time of Chief Nelder's ascension to office, the San Francisco Crime Commission issued its study of the police department, familiarly called the Reichert Report. Each day, Chief Nelder would assemble the department's entire top command staff in the conference room adjoining his office, for what seemed like months on end. There the group assembled sought to refute the report, sentence by sentence, clause by clause, and phrase by phrase. I was called into these meetings from time to time and I remember wondering if all these high-placed officials might not have had something better to do with their time.

Chief Nelder was trying to move the department forward, according to his lights, but there were several factors that stood in the way. For years the Police Association had been an ineffectual company union at best. Since the 1919 Boston Police Strike, which had resulted in the entire Boston police department being fired, police unions were anathema on the American scene. As late as the late 1930s, police association leaders in San Francisco had had to keep their identities secret, for fear of being fired. By the late 60s, as they saw their members being abused under the command of what they saw as ineffectual leadership, police unions around the country began to show their teeth. The unions grew in stridency and became politically active. They demanded, and got, a say in management changes that affected their membership. While these measures improved the officers' lot in some cases, they also sometimes stood in the way of needed reforms. It's axiomatic that the welfare of employees, from a union perspective, is not always consistent with the law enforcement needs of the community.

In 1972, I asked to be transferred to a district station where I would be better positioned to study for the upcoming captain's exam. The work in a district station is as demanding as any in the Hall. From the perspective of somebody studying for a promotional examination, however, the difference in the station is that when your shift was over you could leave your job behind. It didn't matter if the district is on fire, when it was time to get off, your relief took over and you went home. Not so in a staff job in the Hall. There you owned your job, and with no one to relieve you of part of the load, you often found yourself taking it home with you. For that reason, in those days, most successful candidates for promotion came from the night watches in the district stations.

I was thus assigned as a night watch commander at Central Station. I might be prejudiced but on balance I think that might be the best job in the police department. The Central District had it all: Downtown, Chinatown, the Waterfront, North Beach, the Tenderloin and Fisherman's Wharf, the entire spectrum of human folly laid out for your delectation. If you couldn't find something to interest you in the Central you were not alive.

The crazy duty schedule we worked at the time, though, had to have been the worst ever designed by man, both for our health and its effect on family life. We worked one week from 4 to 12 pm and the next week we switched to the midnight to 8 am watch. That means that on one Sunday you would get off at 8 am and return to duty eight hours later at 4 pm. The next week you would get off Saturday night at midnight and return to duty at midnight on Sunday. It was a work schedule designed in hell. No sooner had you gotten used to going to bed after midnight when you were on the 4 to 12, you would switch to midnights the next week which required that you sleep days. Not only was there the switching around but if you were a light sleeper, as I was, the slightest noise would waken you. In my case, I was often unable to get back to sleep and would be grouchy the rest of the day. I have talked to the adult children of police officers whose principal memory of their father was of having to be quiet during the day so as not to waken him.

Even on day duty, I was infrequently home. Because of the commute traffic, I would have to leave for work no later than 7am to be at my desk by 9. I got off at 5 pm but was often held late. And just as well, because the commute at that hour was impossible. The result was that I was gone for 12 hours each day or more. Between the crazy hours, my late-blooming ambition and the demands of duty, I'm sure my family suffered. It's a common enough story and one that I can now regret. I think I should have managed the childrearing part of it better, as others of my colleagues were able to do. I'm proud of my children and the lives they made for themselves.

One dark spot in this period was the corruption investigation in the 1970s mounted by a federal strike force looking into graft charges against the San Francisco police. In an earlier era, San Francisco had been an open town with the blessings of the police, and in accordance with the public will. "(T)here were many upright citizens who had no objection to 'houses' and a bit of gambling," reported former Chief of Police Michael Riordan, speaking in the 1950s of an earlier time. It was alright if San Francisco was "a little crooked." The 1955 Grand Jury report reminded everyone that San Francisco was "not a blue-nose town."

An old sergeant once explained to me the difference between "goodwill money" and graft. I didn't get the distinction at the time and I'm glad. To my relatively simplistic view of the world at the time it was all graft. There is an important distinction. With graft there is some quid pro quo. In return for money or other consideration the official does or does not do something. (It is a common enough system by which much of the world's business gets done on all levels. In Mexico, it's called the *mordido*, or "little bite". In Arab countries it's *backsheesh.* In Chinese treaty ports it was *cumshaw,* for the little gifts that greased the wheels of government. In the U.S. Congress it's called campaign contributions. It is world-wide phenomenon, less prevalent in the United States than elsewhere, and still less prevalent in San Francisco, past and present, than other large cities.)

On the other hand, there are those businesses, those which attract a clientele which might call for a bit more attention from the police, like restaurants and bars, the owners of which actually like to see the police around. These businesses would extend gratuities, often in the form of free meals or meals at a reduced rate. Accepting gratuities was technically against the rules because of the chance that such relationships could cross over the line to become extortion.

It was at Christmas that the gratuity system would truly blossom. Each Christmas, as a matter of course, any number of restaurants or bars would provide bottles to the beat officers, some of which would be passed up the line. Some officers were better than others at seeing that no potential source was overlooked. For myself, I can't say that I turned down reduced cost meals when offered and the odd bottle that came up the line. But I absolutely refused to solicit Christmas bottles when I was on the beat. I saw the delivery of police service as more than that of bellhops or cab drivers or waiters, whose jobs were traditionally rewarded by tips.

(It's ironic that at the time I was at Central, my father was working as a night janitor in a large Kearny Street building. One of his duties was to run the elevator for people who worked late in the building. In that capacity, he made a passing acquaintance with those tenants who worked late. One Christmas, I noticed, he received more bottles as gifts than any police hustler I had ever seen.)

The gratuity system was more extensive at Central than at other stations because that is where bars and restaurants were most highly concentrated among the police districts. And that is what most of the strike force work was about, at least as it related to Central Station. The evidence showed that the gratuity system crossed the line to graft, to include the protection of illegal gambling and prostitution by a couple of section sergeants working the Tenderloin. They and a few patrolmen were convicted of receiving petty graft, and a popular captain, against whom there was really no case, was harassed up to the point of prosecution, and then his charges were dropped.

Commercial vice control is an issue that the city hasn't ever really figured out. Moral and legal considerations aside, it's safe to say, though, that an old-timer would argue that there was certainly less violence, and less female enslavement, associated with organized vice in the old days when the police department was more intimately involved with the seamier side of city life.

17 – In Command

Except for my early stint at Northern Station I had never worked in any of the African-American neighborhoods of the city. I had been detailed to the demonstrations and riots of course, such as they were, and worked for a time on was on the first tactical squad formed in 1967 on which we often found ourselves in black neighborhoods. In Central, that world seemed far removed until one sunny afternoon a bunch of armed Black Panthers showed up on Broadway. That particular incident came to nothing, even as it became clear to me that there were no sanctuaries from the turmoil of the time.

The societal racial divide was brought home to me in a personal way in mid-1973. I was in the midst of studying for captain when I received a call from a study partner who said that the entire process had been brought to a screeching halt. A group of mostly black officers, calling themselves the Officers for Justice, filed a lawsuit claiming that they had been discriminated against in the promotional process, and demanded that they be made captains, As I looked over the list of plaintiffs I saw the names of officers who I hadn't seen at any of the promotional examinations.

Charges of discrimination, claims favoring affirmative action, and assertions of minority "rights" have colored the department from that time to this. A full discussion of the topic goes beyond the scope of a personal memoir. Suffice it to say that in my opinion, and contrary to claims in the suit, minority officers had been advanced to "plum" jobs out of turn, and that is an important factor in explaining their failure to compete in the examinations at that time. (If that assertion seems out-of-step with what now passes for received wisdom, see my full argument at: www.sanfranciscohomicide.com/Stories/Zebra.htm)

Again, I am not going to turn a memoir into a treatise on minority hiring and promotion. On one issue, though, I must rise to the bait. I was brought up to defend my own when wrongly accused. And much of the quest for higher minority representation has come at the expense of the Irish. It is perhaps inevitable that Irish-bashing has come into vogue because of their previous prominence in police affairs. One observer talked about "troglodyte" pockets of "the old-guard, traditionally Irish-Catholic contingent in various stations," who resist the changes that have to be made.

Others cite what they call the "Irish affirmative action" of previous generations as justification for measures which would now exclude the Irish, among other white males, from an equal chance at entry and promotion in public jobs. Contemporary legal reasoning resulting in quotas (or goals) for previous under-represented classes in hiring and promotion is based on the conclusion that a group of white male police officers, often of Irish descent, has somehow manipulated the testing system—a process over which they have no control—to give themselves an advantage in written testing over such disparate groups as women, African-Americans, Asians and Hispanics.

For all my impeccable Irish-Catholic credentials when I joined the department, I never thought for a moment that I would have been appointed had I not measured up to the formal requirements of the job. Many other Irish-Americans at the time did not pass all phases of the examination process, and were not appointed to the job. Likewise, when it came to promotional tests I *know* that I was given no preference over others.

In his ghost-written autobiography, Earl Sanders, the first African-American chief of police and chief complainant in the OFJ lawsuit, blamed many of his problems on an amorphous band of what he calls a "white Irish old-boys network." "In 1973," he claims, "only one man who wasn't Irish had the rank of captain or higher in the SFPD." As a simple matter of fact, at the time of which Sanders writes, the chief and almost all his top staff were demonstrably non-Irish. Does he not remember Police Chief Donald Scott, Deputy Chief William Keays, Supervising Captain Jeremiah Taylor, Director of Criminal Information Louis Feder, Director of Traffic Ignacio Zaragoza, and captains Charles Korelec, Hugh Elbert and Harry Nelson among others, none of whom were Irish?

The Homicide Detail was riddled with Irish old-boy operatives as well, according to Sanders. Again the fact is that Irish-named detectives were a decided minority in the detail at the time. Ironically, it was what he calls an "Irish old-boys network" that had advanced Sanders ahead of his peers in the first place. There is much other ahistorical nonsense in Sanders' book. For instance, he claims that there was once a San Francisco ordinance requiring blacks to step into the gutter when whites passed by. Maybe somewhere, sometime, but not San Francisco.

In these days of acrimonious debate about affirmative action, it seems that an Irish surname can be a downright disadvantage for anyone seeking a career in American law enforcement. When Irish-surnamed Willis Casey was appointed San Francisco police Chief in 1990, he found it necessary to distance himself from his Irish heritage. "I'm one-quarter Irish," he told an interviewer. "My Irish grandfather died in 1901. But people jump to the conclusion that I'm an old Irish cop."

I once gave a talk about the Irish Chiefs of Police in San Francisco to the Irish Literary and Historical Society. One auditor asked during the question period, "Why did you keep the blacks out?" Taken aback, I gave a dismissive answer, but now I would like to take another shot at it: "We didn't. Not in my time."

As circumstances developed, the original injunction against the conduct of the captain's examination was lifted back in 1973, and when the results were published, I had passed first. This was to be the last of the "old" type objective examinations. First, I was assigned as commanding officer of Taraval Station in the Parkside District. There, I witnessed some of the unacknowledged negative consequences of well-intentioned social programming gone wrong. It was about this time that school bussing was implemented to adjust the racial balance in city schools. At the same time, Lincoln High School, a few blocks from Taraval Station, was put on college-like schedule which put students on the street in a strange neighborhood with sometimes multi-hour breaks between classes.

The strong-arm robbery rate went up in the previously peaceable residential area around the school. And the crime pin-map for the district began to show an ever-widening funnel of street crime, starting at Lincoln High and growing wider gradually as it made its way toward the Ocean View District where many of the bussed students lived. Many older Parkside residents, who had walked the neighborhood in safety for many years, were suddenly beaten and robbed in the streets near their homes. The unrecognized, unheralded, and unquantified cost of progress.

On the whole, the Taraval District was the least crime-ridden in the city, so it is ironic that I almost drove into an ambush one day on my way to work. One morning, just after I arrived at work, a call came in about a bank robbery with shots fired. It was a good call and as things turned out it was the Symbionese Liberation Army robbery of the Noriega Street branch of the Hibernia Bank in which heiress Patty Hearst was involved. Just minutes before, I had driven past Noriega Street on 19th Avenue on my way to work. Had the call come in a few minutes earlier than it did, I would have turned right on to Noriega and driven into an ambush set up by a follow-car, positioned behind the gas station across from the bank to take out any police officer who might happen on the scene.

In 1975, I was transferred as commanding officer of Mission Station, a much more active district. As part of the job, I had to interact with the business community, some of whom made me decidedly uncomfortable. Many were solid citizens, but I wondered at the plethora of pawn shops and jewelry stores in such a low income neighborhood. Business is business, but to my mind those operators were victimizing the most vulnerable among us. I had loan-sharked for a while in the army, myself but that was a transaction among equals. Most of the activities of the pawn shops and jewelry stores were technically legal, I suppose, although the proceeds from residential burglaries had a way of getting into the pawn shops with amazing promptitude. I couldn't warm up to people who made their money that way.

The major event in my tenure at the Mission was the police strike. By 1975, the Police Officers Association had grown from a toothless tiger to a political force to be reckoned with. The Board of Supervisors and the Police Officers Association could not agree on the wage package and the officers went out on strike. I was on vacation the week before the strike, so I hadn't been in on the proximate build-up to the job action. I was picked up at my home to go to work that Monday morning by one of the solid sergeants of my command. When he told me that he would vote for the strike, I knew it would happen. I remember being the only captain at that morning's meeting called by the chief who didn't think that the strike talk was all talk. The old guard just didn't believe that the men would walk.

Over the next several days, most of the department was out on strike. Some detectives refrained from joining the strike and in the station all but the captain, the four lieutenants, and a handful of temporary sergeants (who were allowed by the strike committee to continue working so as not to lose their continuity in rank for retirement purposes) went out.

In the first few days, I witnessed the same sort of disorderly phenomenon I had first seen at Fort Campbell in 1955 play itself out again. The striking officers decided to picket the station en masse, for what labor purpose I could never understand. (There was no one to cross the picket-line.) It was more of an excuse to have a party and that's what occurred, not just at Mission but at other stations as well.

One thing I noticed early on. The stabler, solid officers tended to hang back and defer to the self-appointed, more vociferous informal leaders. In the normal course of police business, those who emerged as informal leaders were marginal types. In the confusion of the job action, they came into their own. At Mission Station, they set themselves up as armed perimeter guards, as if someone was going to attack their lines. There were incidents which reflected badly on the professionalism of some. The kooks were in control.

While some officers behaved badly, the regular criminal element was at first quiescent. I went on patrol as did the lieutenant on duty while a sergeant manned the station's phones. It was an eerie feeling to be alone, as I sometimes found myself, the only officer patrolling the district, with nobody to call for back-up. I felt, I thought, as lone sheriffs in western towns of old must have done. There was a tension in the air, a palpable sense of anticipation, an electric waiting for things to come. On the third day or so the atmosphere coalesced. The criminal element came alive. The trouble started with several storefront burglaries, the perpetrators of one of which drove an auto through a front window. There was talk that the Highway Patrol would be invited in to patrol the city streets.

That didn't happen because Mayor Joseph Alioto intervened and settled the strike in favor of employee demands. There were those at the time who criticized the mayor for caving in to pressure. As one who was in the district where the tension was brewing, I applauded his action. If the Highway Patrol had been introduced to patrol the city streets, I firmly believed that there would have been violence between them and the striking officers. Given the climate at the time, it would have taken the army to restore order. I'm one of those who believe that for all the complex institutional societal protections with which we have surrounded ourselves, there is but a thin layer of civilization to protect us from our baser instincts. And those instincts lay in waiting, always poised to emerge.

18 – Me and Charlie Gain

When I did my first tour of duty at Richmond Station in the 1960s, I had noticed that the walls of the old stable building at the rear of the stationhouse were lined with shelving, inexplicably containing a variety of used vehicular parts such as one would find in an auto repair shop. When I returned to the station in 1980, the same used parts were still there. It was not until I retired and started researching the department's history that the mystery was solved. Richmond Station had been the headquarters of the department's motorcycle unit in 1912. For all those long intervening decades, the abandoned parts had remained in their place and no one had taken the initiative to clear them out. The words "curiosity" and "change" were not prominent in our organizational lexicon.

That was not an isolated incident. Examples of organizational inertia abounded. In 1960, I had noticed mug books of arrested criminals dating from the 1930s strewn around the assembly room at Central Station, and at Mission Station in 1975, reports from long-retired officers about suspected World 2 German collaborators from the early 1940s were scattered about.

Even as a foot patrol officer on the midnight in the Richmond District, I had realized that the idea of walking around all night looking for broken store windows was an absurd waste of manpower. Yet no one thought to change the system. All bureaucracies resist change, to be sure, but in our case it had gotten ridiculous. I came to realize that what you do when you tell someone to change the way he's been doing his job for a period of time, is communicating to him that he has been doing it wrong all along, and, incidentally, that he wasn't smart enough to realize it. Its bad in any institution, but in government, where there is really no financial bottom line, conditions can calcify into organizational paralysis.

The agents of the department's reluctance to change, as things unfolded, were the very same old-time gentlemen who had welcomed me to the job. The problem was not theirs alone; it was rooted in the civic culture of the town. Nineteenth Century San Francisco—during the period when the department was formed—was the tenth largest city in the nation, and the only one of the ten west of the Mississippi. Many of the departmental practices were modeled on those of the large cities of the East, particularly New York City. San Francisco was a big city when Los Angeles was a still a wide spot in the road.

So, in the early 20th century, when modern management practices were developed, growing California cities like Los Angeles, San Diego and even Oakland began to adopt the basic business practices which are fundamental to any efficiently run organization. San Francisco, however, where we knew how to do everything already, stood aloof, thus assuring its place in the time warp in which it found itself. (Retired Chief Tom Cahill told me once that when he went to address a group of North Bay law enforcement officers, he was welcomed as a representative of the "Republic of San Francisco.")

As I studied for the various promotional exams, I became aware that what the management books had to say about police practices were alien to us as an organization. I mentioned some of the seeming lapses to the bosses and was told that "that was all theory." Never mind that what we were doing was also based on theory, albeit one not supported by any modern management philosophy. And some of the new theory looked pretty good to me. In my brief stint in the Investigations Bureau, I noticed that there was no system of case control, as called for in "the books." When I mentioned to my boss that the cases were assigned out to the detectives without any mechanism to check whether any work had been done on them, he told me that if anyone complained, the errant Inspectors would be disciplined. I thought we could be a bit more proactive than that. Investigative case management systems had been described as far back as the 1934 *Municipal Police Administration,* so it wasn't anything necessarily cutting-edge that we needed to do Most of the officers and detectives, to be sure, were dedicated, smart, hard-working people who had just not been given the proper tools to do the job right.

It was into such an environment that an outsider, Charles Gain, former chief of Oakland, was appointed Chief of Police. When he interviewed captains for the top positions I didn't make the cut. My Irish name and mug probably worked against me with a man who spent his career hearing that the

SFPD was run by an Irish Mafia. I was moved from Mission Station to Planning, a second string job in the San Francisco ranking of positions at the time, but one that the chief valued highly as I came to learn.

The informal organization went after him. Chief Gain wasn't just an outsider but one with a suspiciously liberal bent. His enemies checked and found that his driver's license had recently expired, a misdemeanor which police-friendly journalists published with glee. He was criticized for changing the color of the police cars from manly black to "baby blue." (I notice that New York police cars are now colored white with pronounced "baby blue" stripes and logo.)

Chief Gain was castigated for moving the ceremonial American flag out of his inner office to the public reception area, the clear implication being that he was less than completely patriotic. Had his critics known of his war record, perhaps they wouldn't have been so quick to judge him on that score. (Among the members of the 29th Infantry Division who went ashore on Omaha Beach on June 6, 1944 was a young enlisted man named Charles Gain. He was to fight with his unit across the hedgerows of Normandy to the break-out at St. Lo, earning two bronze stars along the way.) He isn't one to trumpet his own accomplishments and I don't think the informal organization at the time was of a mood to give him a break anyway.

In truth, I must admit, he didn't always help his own cause. An Okie Era immigrant from West Texas in the 1930s, and subsequently rejected by his neighbors after he arrived, he grew up poor among Oakland blacks. That experience imbued him with a righteous sense of justice. Even his severest critics have to admit he is fair to a fault. Coupled with his orneriness, he is actually a retiring, almost shy man with strangers, a trait which his detractors construed as contempt. A "hail fellow well met" he was not.

In my new position at planning, I had occasion to work closely with the chief, and for the first time I saw a way out of the organizational quandary we faced in the department: how to move out of the past where we were mired, into a present that would be better for everyone. In a word, I supported Chief Gain's efforts to bring the department up to date and that didn't go over well with those of my fellows who were satisfied that things should remain just the way they were. In a stroke, he got rid of the nineteenth century organizational structure over which the department had been agonizing for years. He established the first real field training program in the Police Academy. He also established a rational mechanism for issuing written orders out of the chaotic mess which preceded it. He dragged the Property Clerk's office into the twentieth century by taking it off of the cash basis on which it had operated and introduced the unit to the check book. He also put an end to on-duty drinking. The changing civic environment, and Supervising Captain Jeremiah Taylor, had already brought much of it to an end. But he put the nail in its coffin. Some of the changes he implemented would save many later bosses untold grief as they tried to function in a very different and more highly scrutinized San Francisco from that which they had known.

For all its civic insularity, the San Francisco Police Department was not, and is not, an institutional basket case. Its peacekeeping model of policing had strengths not to be so much found in the law enforcement model departments with which it was often compared. While Los Angeles officers might be more technically proficient in many areas, they were also known for certain heartlessness in dealing with the public. San Francisco police were known for "sending the drunk home," rather than necessarily locking him up, to solving neighborhood problems rather than just putting someone in jail. This difference in attitudes toward the public may have contributed to the more virulent strain of public disorders occurring in other cities. San Francisco detectives, while perhaps somewhat deficient in managing case information effectively, sometimes showed marvelously intuitive individual imagination in solving knotty cases. Chief Gain's idea was to keep what was best in the old system and to add what was new and needed: to create a technically proficient, humane police force.

In February 1977, I was appointed to the position of deputy chief for Administration. In that position I worked even closer with the chief, particularly on the management overhaul. Personally, it was a very trying time.

Figure 16-The Deputy Chief.

I remember meeting a fellow officer from my Richmond station days after I was appointed chief. His comment, evidently reflecting his perception about the demands of the job, was "Now you've got it made. You don't have to do anything." I had never worked harder in my life.

Something always has to give, and it this instance it was my family. My children were entering their teen-aged years with all the angst that I should have remembered so well, and I suspect I wasn't always there for them on a personal basis. Our Christine was a competitive ice skater during those years whose competitions we followed around the state. We depleted our ready cash reserves, and maxed out the VISA card, to get Davitt one of the early high-cost personal computers so he could explore his dream. It was a sound investment as his success with Microsoft has proved. All in all though, I suspect I came across day-to-day as something of a soulless authority figure, who floated in most nights to make a few pronouncements and was gone again early the next day.

It was during Chief Gain's term that the provisions of the settlement of the OFJ lawsuit were thrashed out to much sound and fury. Depositions were taken. Charles Gain was in the middle of all that and I got to watch him up close. To his detractors he was ready to hand the department over to minorities. Yet I watched as he refused other city officials' offers to design tests which would have assured minority representation without reference to qualifications. "No," he said. "We want the minorities but they must be otherwise qualified."

It was he, alone among others, who abolished the largely African American Community Relations Unit because they were not doing any community relations. It was on his watch that the Board of Supervisors finally agreed to a settlement on the OFJ suit. We can—and I do—criticize some of the provisions of that settlement, how they came to be, and actions that have flowed from it, but no chief since has seen fit to take a substantially different position. In sum, it would have been better, to my mind, if they could have achieved their intended ends without demonizing other people who had nothing to do with their situation.

Because of his liberal orientation, many thought that Chief Gain was soft on crime. Not so. He had a crime control program not unlike the fabled COMSTAT now being trumpeted about, which targeted high crime areas and placed resources there to stamp it out. His program—and indeed COMSTAT which is now looked on as the solution to all that ills American cities—was actually a variation on crime control practices developed in Los Angeles in the 1950s.

Charles Gain really angered the troops, though, when he said he would hire homosexuals as police officers.

19 – White Night

Harvey Milk used to visit me in my office at Mission Station when I was captain there in the middle 70's. That was before he was the Harvey Milk of legend. One day I noticed that he was wearing a belt buckle with a hard-hat deep-sea diver's emblem on its face. I asked him what that was all about, and he told me that he had been a diver in the Navy. Once, as he recounted it, he was deep below the surface of the sea when he suffered a temporary loss of air due to a kinked hose or some other malfunction. His first thought, he said, was "They found out!"

Revisionist commentators have sometimes reported that there was much tension between the gay and police communities at the time. There were the usual stresses which occur with any community seeking more protection. There were the frequent attacks by gay-bashers, and the demands from the community that we do more. There had been enforcement efforts in the 1950s and 1960s to enforce laws against cross-dressing, to be sure, but I didn't sense any manifest hostility to gays. It was more the enforcement of an older civic code ordered by the old timers. It is useful to remember that one of the reasons for the large gay community in San Francisco is the very tolerance that had drawn them here in the first place. By the mid 1970s the relations between the Gay community and the officers at Mission Station were pretty good for the most part, at least until White Night in 1979. Indeed we conducted an annual softball game between the Gay community in the Castro and the officers at Mission Station.

On November 27, 1978, former Supervisor Dan White entered City Hall where he murdered the Mayor and Supervisor Milk. White, who had most recently been a member of the fire department, had also once been a police officer. Thereafter the relationship between the Gay community and some elements of the police department did begin to erode. In the immediate aftermath of Moscone's murder, Dianne Feinstein was appointed mayor. As a member of the Board of Supervisors, Feinstein had never been particularly chummy with Chief Gain. Her sentiments seemed to lie closer to those of the Police Association. Yet she kept Chief Gain on, doubtless recognizing his abilities as a manager. I was transferred from the head of Administration to the head of Field Operations with responsibility for the nine district stations, the Traffic Division and other patrol related units.

White was arrested shortly after the killings and in April 1979 was placed on trial in Superior Court on what most saw as a double premeditated first degree murder. It looked like a slam dunk. On May 21, the manslaughter verdict—based on what was called a "twinky defense," that White's mental depression had been aggravated by an excessive intake of sugar—was announced. Members of San Francisco's gay community, along with many straights, were stunned beyond belief. To the public mind, the verdict was absurd. The psychiatrist who attributed White's actions to his depressive state was roundly criticized. (Not to excuse White for what he did, but it is pretty well established that the anger generated during a depressive episode can be directed outward as well as toward oneself.)

The verdict was announced shortly after 5 p.m., inconveniently just after the entire police department day watch had reported off duty. Without any firm knowledge about when the jury deliberations would end, we had no plan in place. (Since the Los Angeles riots following the verdict in the Rodney King beating case, in 1992, the announcements of jury verdicts in potentially volatile cases are often delayed until police can make the necessary arrangements.)

We had been assured that day by leaders of the Castro community that there would be no difficulty if a verdict lesser than murder came in because it would be "counterproductive" (their word). Shortly after 5 pm, one of those same leaders was seen inciting the patrons out of Castro Street bars to march on City Hall.

A group formed up at Castro and Market, as they had so many times before, and proceeded to march to City Hall. There were reports along the line of march that the crowd was mostly peaceable with some violent elements. I had the dubious honor of being the sole uniformed officer on the steps of City Hall when the marchers arrived at the Polk Street side. Finding nothing to distract them from their outrage, the mob began to attack the face of the building. The chief soon joined me from home. We called for reinforcements but while they were marshalling, the crowd took over the steps and began beating on the glass doors of city hall.

As our forces began streaming in, the crowd continued to beat on the doors. The tactical unit, then coming on duty with 30 officers, was immediately available for deployment. Fearing that the crowd would get inside and damage the main frame computers in the basement, we violated a basic Von Clausewitz rule and split our forces, sending the tactical unit to enter the Van Ness Street side of the building to confront the mob from the inside.

We continued to call up reserves from home and made impromptu efforts to engage the mob with speakers sympathetic to their cause. In the late 1960s, in the midst of the anti-war demonstrations of that era, the department acquired a surplus military loudspeaker called a loudhailer. The self-contained, battery-operated unit could be heard a mile away. Early in the disorder, I put in a call for the loudhailer to be delivered to City Hall. As luck would have it—or was it just the usual organizational ineffectiveness?—nobody on duty knew where it was stored.

In the meantime, we asked Supervisor Carol Ruth Silver to address the mob from the balcony in front of the Mayor's Office with a police bullhorn. Supervisor Silver, a sympathetic figure to those below, began to speak. The crowd applauded respectfully. For a time peace held the upper hand. In the end, the bullhorn was too feeble to be heard below. The rock throwing resumed. The violence built until almost 11 p.m., when several police cars parked along McAllister Street were set afire by rioters. It was only then that we swept Civic Center Plaza and chased rioters as they trashed shop windows on Market Street and in the surrounding area.

Many of the rioters returned triumphantly to the Castro district, followed by a number of very angry officers. Early on May 22, a squad of police officers entered the Elephant Walk bar at 18th and Castro (the exact location where I had pulled the fire alarm in 1942) and routed the patrons in what many saw as a retaliatory "police riot." The events of the night were capped by a police withdrawal from the Castro, dubbed "Mullen's Retreat" in my honor by officers who would have preferred a more forceful outcome.

Much of the after-action criticism centered on tactics and timing as the reasons for what went wrong. Some said we moved against the crowd too late, unnecessarily endangering officers who were forced to stand in formation in front of the rock-throwing mob. Others complained that when we did move, officers used excessive force. There could be no way of reconciling the views of those at opposite ends of the opinion spectrum.

Preliminary to my decision to withdraw the officers from the Castro, all was confusion on the scene. The mob held the intersection in which city busses were trapped, and groups of officers were intermingled with the crowd. I specifically remember two men in fairy costumes, one magenta and the other mint green, complete with wands and lace wings, dancing in the street behind where I was standing. Where these guys had come from on an early Tuesday morning I have no idea, but it was plain to me that our formations had been compromised.

At the time, friends on the scene reminded me that if I pulled out, my future career prospects would be ruined. In full recognition of that reality, I ordered the withdrawal. I have no regrets; it was the right thing to do. In later years, other friends trying to justify my decision to withdraw from the Castro pointed to other instances - more common than is supposed - when officers have withdrawn from the field in the face of overwhelming odds. That wasn't the case that night at all. Having come through more than decade of assaults on their values and their lives, during which 14 of their fellow officers were murdered, the officers' blood was up. It wasn't a question of protecting the officers from the crowd. It was the reverse.

As the officers moved up Castro Street, followed by a jeering mob, I was standing in front of the Castro Theater. One of the crowd broke away and approached within 20 feet of me, where he loudly denounced me as a "pig-faced Irish motherfucker" before scurrying back to the safety of the mob. Truth to tell, the last thing I expected from that crowd was an ethnic slur. And the irony wasn't lost on me that my withdrawal order, which even then I knew would cost me dearly in the opinion of working cops, had also saved my detractor from getting his butt kicked by some very angry police officers.

It was a chaotic period in civic life. With a mayoral election coming in the Fall, the political knives were out. Charles Gain was on his way out and it looked as if I was going to join him. Though it wasn't known generally, I knew that the new chief was to be Commander Cornelius Murphy who worked under me in Field Operations at the time. Our relationship was good.

Before I departed from the scene, I had a chance to reprise my actions with a similar outcome, which again earned me the scorn of those who would like a more forceful resolution to crowd problems. My actions also may have facilitated Dianne Feinstein's election in the proximate mayoral election, though that isn't why I did it. It was Halloween, and the mayoral election, at which Dianne Feinstein would run for the office on her own, was just a few days off. Tensions were high that year between the police and Gays at the annual Halloween celebration in the Castro because of the bad feelings on both sides after the White Night debacle.

I had my command post in the Fire Department Credit Union overlooking Market and Castro streets, the center of the revelry. As the party was breaking up in the early morning hours of the next day there was that usual bar-closing tension, multiplied by the vastly greater numbers involved. Some of the crowd started walking away down Market and others could be seen walking up the hill at 17th Street.

At that point, the police captain in charge of the Tactical Division took it upon himself to march his company and take up a position in the middle of the intersection at 17th and Market. I watched as the people turned back up Market Street and down 17th, presumably to watch the fun. I ordered the captain to march his troops right back out of there and he did so, to the accompaniment of comments over the police radio that "He's done it again," with reference to me. But the crowds again dispersed and things ended peacefully. Dianne Feinstein won the mayoralty that year in a close election, and that might not well have happened if there had been more disorder in the Castro on Halloween.

In the end, the informal organization would prevail. Feinstein said it was easier to replace a coach than an entire team. Chief Gain was out, and so was I. Actually, I was asked to stay on in my position as deputy chief. Feinstein made it a precondition for exempt rank officers to live within the city limits, however. Jeannie and I looked at houses in the city but in the end we decided that given our family situation with two children established in high school life elsewhere, it would on balance be too disruptive generally. So I reverted to my civil service rank of captain and was assigned to Richmond Station.

But I was given one last insight before heading for the fog belt. On New Year's Eve everybody worked, as was customary. I was still deputy chief, though I had but a few days left on my term. That night I went about checking the various district events so as to reallocate forces should it become necessary. We don't hear of the riots that don't happen. Midnight found me in the Castro at 18th when the Gay residents of the neighborhood took it in their heads to take over the intersection, much as they had on White Night, albeit in a more festive mood. The officer in charge of the scene, a well respected hard-line street cop—and a man who had been present on White Night and later criticized me for letting them have the street—chose to let them have the street himself, so, he said, as not to embarrass the incoming chief with a ruckus. It's not always what you do that's important, but who does it.

In January 1980 I reverted to my civil service rank of captain and was assigned to Richmond Station where I went to lick my psychic wounds. Not much was expected of district captains in those days. (From what I can see, station captains are now much more involved with their communities than we were.) So I set about implementing some of my ideas on a minor scale, the details of which would probably be of little interest to a non-specialist reader.

After a time, I was looking for more action so I asked to be transferred to a busier downtown station where a vacancy had occurred. Instead I met Chief Murphy at a banquet and he asked me to come to the Hall and set up an inspection unit to look at department procedures and practices as to their adequacy and compliance. A non-sexy but important subject which had long interested me. It still does.

The old systems were ingrained, though, and the practitioners were not always amenable to change. With Chief Murphy's backing, I was able to revise the written directive system out of its antiquated sorry state. It's not a very glamorous subject even though it's important to the effective management of the department. I also developed the first comprehensive written crowd management procedures for the department.

When the National Democratic Convention came to town in 1984, I was put in charge of the security planning which included liaison with other law enforcement agencies as well as Democratic Party operatives and other national political leaders. In the course of those efforts, I was reappointed to the position of deputy chief, the restriction requiring city residence having been relaxed. Also, I like to think, I was needed downtown.

Thereafter, I organized an Information Systems Management Division with overall responsibility for the departmental computer operations with an emphasis on developing management information systems to assist with the better management of department operations. Before that project was fairly started, the department administration changed and I retired. And from what I hear, the information management systems are still pretty much what they were that day.

Afterword

In January 1986, Chief Con Murphy retired and was replaced by Frank Jordan. Jordan was agreeable to my continuing in my position—at least he told me so—but most of the others he chose for the top positions would not be comfortable working with me. Had I returned to my civil service rank of captain, which was what was in store for me, it would have reduced my ultimate retirement benefits. So, I opted to retire which I did on January 16.

Part of Jordan's top staff's discomfort, I'm sure, had to do with my position as a vocal agent for change. There was something else going on as well. The people selected for the top slots were contemporaries of mine. We had entered the department at about the same time. But as things developed, I was promoted more swiftly then they. I was being promoted to captain and deputy chief while some of them were trying to figure out how to make lieutenant. If you want to make an enemy, I can't think of any better way.

There was more to it than that. I had collaborated with the enemy in the person of Chief of Police Charles Gain. Never mind that organizational performance improved under his guidance. He was an outsider and was to be shunned. All institutions have their informal rules which one violates at his peril. Police departments, even more than other groups, have a strong tribal component. (Other institutions have presidents, CEOs, managers, or superintendents. Police departments have "Chiefs", a word denoting police origins in an earlier, less complicated time.)

Tribal traits, like unswerving and unquestioning adherence to the personified will of the group, can be very effective on offense: when going through the door on a dope raid, or when working together against a larger hostile crowd. But the same traits don't always result in the best outcomes when operating in a complex modern environment, say figuring out the best deployment plan to match the needs of the public being served. The stubborn contrary kid in me eventually declined to go along with the old, ineffective tribal ways and for that I was made to pay. So be it.

There was a part of me that wanted out anyway. Given the nature of the department culture, we ran from one crisis to the next. Instead of systematizing solutions to problems to assure that they did not reoccur, we would put on a temporary patch and move on to the next pressing issue. By 1986 I was frustrated, tired, and bored from continuously revisiting the same issues, time after time.

Retirement was something of a psychic wrench. For the institutionalized individual, whether prisoner, soldier, or civil servant, it's a tough adjustment to make: to figure out what you should do when you get up in the morning. I had long been interested in the criminal justice history of the West and indeed had had a couple of journal pieces published while I was still working. So, when I retired, I set out to research and write a book on the establishment of the justice system in San Francisco during the Gold Rush years. It was published in 1989 by the University of Nevada Press as *Let Justice Be Done: Crime and Politics in Early San Francisco.*

About that time, I was invited to submit opinion pieces by the opinion page editor of the old *San Francisco Examiner*—and later the Hearst *Chronicle.* The thrust of the articles was mainly historical, sometimes with a contemporary hook as dictated by events occurring in the news. That led me to keep abreast of departmental affairs more, I expect, than most retirees. And that's how I have spent my time since then, writing articles for the local dailies which sometimes remind current management how things need to be done. Many of the pieces, keyed to recurring press revelations about failures in departmental management systems, included suggestions about how to make things work better. It seems that now (2009), with the appointment of yet another outside chief, some of those systems will finally be introduced. Along the way, I wrote several more books about the history of San Francisco's justice system.

Our children are now raised and off making successful lives of their own. Our grandchildren, as they do, fill our hearts with joy, and hopes for the future. Their childhood is far different from anything I knew, and that is just fine with me. Our life is placid now, except for the occasional crises of the younger members which are part of every family life. I meet frequently with friends for lunch these days where we learnedly disagree about all these things, and comment on the moves of the current dancers from the security of the shade beneath the roadside tree.

It's no longer the San Francisco of my youth. Physically, the city is a much more beautiful place than it ever was. Looking at an aerial view of the city now compared to an earlier time, one will notice first that the city is covered with street trees where once it looked like a barren waste. Pleasant sidewalk cafes now grace the same streets where they were once forbidden, for no good reason that I can discern.

Downtown is being revitalized and a whole new neighborhood is growing up in what was once on its way to becoming a South of Market slum. Women no longer wear gloves and hats with veils when they go downtown. And bars are no longer pressured to close on Good Friday from 12 to 3. It's a much changed city, as is the way of the world, although it happened here faster and more dramatically than many other places.

As I walk around downtown San Franciscan these days, perhaps stopping at the great little bistro on Union Square, I am surrounded by the sounds of tourist languages from around the world. And the larger body of San Franciscans, at all levels, come in every shape and hue, with Asians moving to perhaps supplant non-Latino whites as the most numerous group in the city. The Irish still aren't off the hook. Recently, the president of the Police Commission was quoted as saying that graduates of St. Ignatius and Sacred Heart high schools need not expect anymore to be appointed to the civil service exempt positions in the higher reaches of the police department.

For myself, the sometimes impressionable if mischievous youngster of my youth has become the amusedly skeptical old man of today. The shut-down little 5 year-old of 1940 has somehow made it to 73 and the year 2009. Sometimes along the way, I wasn't always sure that I would make it that far. Regrets? I suppose so, and there are some things I would have handled differently. As was my practice in school, I didn't always try as hard as I might have. But, for all of that, in my judgment, I think I did OK. Even if not, there is nothing that can be changed now.

As mentioned at the outset, I started to put together these thoughts for the benefit of my grandchildren when they are older and I am gone. I was hurried along in that effort by a medical diagnosis which assures I won't be here then. All of which brings to mind one last childhood memory. It was the custom in Rose Smith's household, as in many Irish Catholic families at the time, to say the rosary each night after dinner. (It was a custom which harked back to the Penal Days in Ireland when it was illegal to practice the Catholic faith openly.) We all knelt against the dining room chairs around the table, and dutifully "told our beads" as Rose Smith intoned the mysteries of the rosary. She would then recite the Litany of the Saints, and remember those already departed by name. Her final prayer contained what to my young mind was an inherent contradiction. She would close the proceedings with a prayer asking for a "happy death." How can a death be happy, my younger self reasoned? Now, having observed as many have passed along, I can fully understand what she meant.

The world belongs to the current generation, Thomas Jefferson told us, and that's what we are seeing. The new world cannot truly be born until the old one dies. Much of the tension in the last several decades can be viewed in a broader sense as the inevitable eruption in a long-simmering conflict between the San Francisco that had been, and city that was about to be, the death throes of the old San Francisco, you might say, amid the birthing pains of the new. Whatever happens, it will be a world which no one today can predict with any degree of certainty—if history is any judge of such things.

We can only hope that the more recent arrivals to San Francisco remember that they came from someplace worse; and on their arrival, they received a more welcoming reception than they could have expected elsewhere. And while they build their own San Francisco memories, we can hope they respect the memories of those who went before. These have been mine.

LaVergne, TN USA
01 December 2009
165706LV00001B/104/P

9 781602 644632